# Impact of Tantra on Religion and Art

Tantra in Contemporary Researches, no. 1

# Impact of Tantra on Religion and Art

T.N. Mishra

D.K. Printworld (P) Ltd.
NEW DELHI-110015

**Cataloging in Publication Data — DK**

Mishra, T. N. (Tej Narain), 1945-
Impact of tantra on religion and art.
(Tantra in contemporary researches, no. 1).
Includes bibliographical references (p. ).
Includes index.

1. Art, Tantric. 2. Tantric Buddhism.
3. Tantrism. I. Title. II. Series : Tantra in contemporary researches, no. 1.

**ISBN 81-246-0073-2**

*First Published in India in 1997*



*Published by:*
**D.K. Printworld (P) Ltd.**
*Regd. office* : 'Sri Kunj', F-52, Bali Nagar
New Delhi - 110 015
*Phones* : (011) 545 3975, 546-6019; *Fax* : (011) 546-5926

*Printed by* : D P's Impressive Impressions, New Delhi - 110059

# Preface

TANTRA, as widely accepted nowadays, refers to a body of literature that spreads, in particular, knowledge of profound things through the aid of *yantra* or mystic diagrams, and *mantra*, words possessing esoteric meanings, with the ultimate aim of salvation. It is interesting to note that it is later literature, from the fifth or sixth century onwards, that refers to *Tantra* as a special religious or philosophical concept; the term *Tantra* is rather used in a non-religious and ordinary sense in the different philosophical systems prior to that time. The word *Tantra*, at one time, could be applied to the sacred literature of the Vaiṣṇavites and the Śaivites as well though, again, it is now applied solely for the religious literature of the *Śāktas*. The religion and philosophy of the *Tantra* made a strong impact not only on the religious systems of Brāhmaṇical Hinduism, Buddhism and Jainism but also, on the art and architectural forms of the time.

The Tāntric religion, essentially, accords supreme importance to the body. It maintains that the elements comprising the body cannot be dissociated from the environmental elements so that the laws governing the latter may be applied to the body to bring its elements into some kind of order. It emphasises the practical mode of realising the nature of Reality. This practical aspect involves *sādhanā*, an essential part of the Tāntric life. Tantrism is associated with two aspects — the sophisticated and the popular, of which the former involves many Brāhmaṇical Hindu elements. An important one is the concept of *śakti* (energy). *Śakti* is found in the body as the serpent power or *kuṇḍalinī* within the *mūlādhāra cakra*. It is only by awakening the dormant female energy by yogic exercises and lifting her up through the regions of the five other *cakras* to the realm of *sahasrāra* that a *sādhaka* can achieve salvation. The Tāntric concept views the act of creation as a result of the union of the Female and Male Principles, the former being the more important functionary.

My earlier writings were largely concerned with the historical romance of the *Tantra*. The study undertaken here, however, does not deal with the history of Tāntric beliefs and practices as such; it is rather an attempt to introduce *Tantra* in a different perspective, with a specific viewpoint.

This book covers various aspects of Tāntric religion, philosophy and art including evolution of the *Tantra*, fundamental concepts of the *Tantra*, the tremendous impact of *Tantra* on Brāhmaṇical Hinduism, Buddhism and Jainism, and the Tāntric influence in art and architecture.

The chapters are thematically arranged and they deal with the subject within the span of a wide mosaic. The Tāntric religion is extremely interesting: it is mysterious, it provokes curious enquiries, its messages are full of esoteric meanings and its symbols are adequately meaningful. Here, I have tried to explain some of its mysteries and point out certain misconceptions prevailing in the society about Tāntric religion and its practices.

In the collection of relevant material for this volume, I am indebted to many scholars and institutions. Of these, mention may particularly be made of those scholars whose published books and articles were consulted during the preparation of this volume, and others who supplied me unpublished information during discussions that contributed to the formation of my ideas. I am very much indebted to my spiritual teacher for his help and guidance for over a decade. I am equally grateful to other *ācāryas* and saints for their guidance and suggestions.

I am thankful to Dr. T.K. Biswas, Joint Director, Bharat Kala Bhavan, Banaras Hindu University who studied the manuscript and made valuable suggestions. I am obliged to Dr. Deena Bandhu Pandey, Reader, Department of History of Art, B.H.U. and all my colleagues at Bharat Kala Bhavan, B.H.U. for their help in the preparation of this book.

My thanks are also due to Bharat Kala Bhavan Library, Philosophy Department of B.H.U., Central Library of B.H.U., Saraswati Pustakalaya, Sampurnanand Sanskrit Viswavidyalaya (Varanasi), and to some personal libraries.

I also wish to mention here the moral support I received from my wife, Vandana Mishra and my daughters, Kavita, Pratima and Jyoti in the course of preparing this volume.

**T.N. Mishra**

# Contents


| | | |
|---|---|---|
| | *Preface* | 5 |
| | *List of Illustrations* | 11 |
| 1. | Introduction | 17 |
| 2. | Religious Mythology | 23 |
| 3. | The Concept of the *Tantra* | 35 |
| 4. | Philosophy of the *Tantra* and *Sādhanā* | 43 |
| 5. | Evolution of the *Tantras* | 53 |
| 6. | Concept of Śakti and Śāktism | 63 |
| 7. | Tāntric Culture of Buddhism and its Tenets | 79 |
| 8. | *Siddhi, Siddha* and the *Nātha* Cult | 91 |
| 9. | Influence of *Tantra* in Art | 97 |
| | *Visuals* | 113 |
| | *Bibliography* | 145 |
| | *Glossary* | 155 |
| | *Index* | 173 |

# List of Illustrations

1. *Mṛtyuñjaya-Śiva* (Conqueror of Death) — Basohli (Mankot), *ca.* AD 1715, Bharat Kala Bhavan, Varanasi.

2. *Hiraṇyagarbha* (Cosmic Egg) — An illustration from *Bhāgavata Purāṇa*, Basohli, *ca.* AD1730, Bharat Kala Bhavan, Varanasi.

   *hiraṇyagarbha samavartāgre*
   *bhūtasya jātaḥ patireka āsita*
   *sa dādhāra pṛthvī dyāmutemā*
   *kasmai devāya haviṣā vidhāma?*
   (*Ṛgveda*, X.121.1)

   Hiraṇyagarbha was produced in the beginning; he was born as sole lord of all beings. He held the earth, the sky and all these. What god (except Him) should we worship with oblation?

3. *Śiva-Śakti* — Śiva manifests Himself before Kṛṣṇa and chief priest, Mandi, *ca.* AD 1790, Bharat Kala Bhavan, Varanasi.

   "What need have I of any outer woman, I have an 'Inner woman' within myself". Kuṇḍalinī is the 'Inner woman', she effulgents as millions of suns flashing in the centre of the *sādhaka*'s body.

4. *Chinnamastā* — Rajasthan, Late 18th century AD, Bharat Kala Bhavan, Varanasi.

   Chinnamastā signifies the transcendental power of

will and vision. The goddess sits on Rati and Kāma, who personify the primordial desire which gives rise to all creation. The garland of *muṇḍamālā* symbolizes wisdom and power of *rajoguṇa*, the kinetic force which gives impetus to all activities. Sword that severs her own head are the symbols of dissolution and annihilation directing the *sādhaka* to shed his sense of ego; in her destructive and creative aspects she signifies apparent dissolution and return to the elements and reconstitution into other forms. Thus, the process of being is an unbroken, infinite one. She is naked (*digambarī*— space clad), full breasted but her womb is the sphere of endless creation and dissolution.

Her third eye looks beyond space and time. She is the changeless, limitless primordial power creating the great drama. She is also known as Mahādevī, Kālikā because she is without any beginning or end; her body is the all-pervading blue colour of the universe. Though herself changeless, she binds all beings (Śiva) by way of Māyā. She is the sole creator, perserver and destroyer of infinite millions of worlds; her nakedness symbolises creation, her full and high breasts denote preservation, her true nature stand for eternal liberation.

The union of male and female principles is a symbol of eternal communion and an awareness of oneness through duality. The conjunction of opposites as Rati and Kāma, male and female represents transcending of the phenomenal and abolition of all experience of duality. From the Tāntric point of view, the consummation is the human being, man and woman comprised as one unit. Nothing dies in the world; what is apparently dead returns to its elements and then again is reconstructed into form. There is one unbroken, infinite process of life and change. An element may start in the sun and ultimately enter a human being, an animal or plant on earth; only the name and form differ.

Rati and Kāma represent kinetic energy. Kāma is the god of love about whom it is said in *Rgveda*: 'Desire first arose at the dawn of creation". In the *Atharvaveda*, Kāma is known as the creation. They remain in a union of oneness, enjoying that supreme bliss (*paramānanda*) which is the highest non-duality.

This form of union is known as *yuganaddha*. The absolute unification of all duality is the real principle of union which has been termed as *yuganaddha* in Buddhist-tantra. It is said that through the purging of the two motions of creative process and absolute cessation, the state of unity called *yuganaddha* is attained. There is neither affirmation nor denial, neither purity nor impurity, neither form nor formlessness; it is a synthesis of such duality.

5. *Śiva-Liṅga* — 7th or 8th century AD; Kaśmīr, stone, Bharat Kala Bhavan, Varanasi.

The *liṅga*, the aniconic symbol (*avyakta rūpa*) reflects the presence of invisible transcendental reality of Śiva. There is no object in this world more sacred than the *liṅga*. The *liṅga* stands erect (*ūrdhva liṅga*), it's top pointing upwards as if ready to shed seed; yet by yogic discipline it restrains and retains the potent substance.

The *mukha-liṅga* (one, four or five faces) stands for Śiva's partly symbolic and partly represented forms (*vyakta*). Descending from its apex in the four directions of space, the *liṅga* in its complex system of analogical categories embodies the five elements, ether, air, fire, water and earth, or the five senses, sound, taste, touch, form and smell which are personified in the *pañcamukhaliṅga* as *iśāna*, *aghora*, *sadyojāta*, *vāmadeva* and *tatapuruṣa*. Śiva manifested himself in human form (*vyakta*) also as one who sets everything in motion and is always dancing, absorbed in yoga or enjoying supreme bliss.

6. *Yoni-Paṭṭa* — Metal, Temple object, Varanasi.

7. *Prajñapāramitā*—Probably 13th century AD from Chandi Sari temple, Jāvā (Indonesia), stone.

8. *A Devotee with Śiva-Liṅga*—Stone, Gupta Period, 6th century AD, Ḅharat Kala Bhavan, Varanasi.

9. *Oṁ — Ca.* AD 1810, Pahari, Bharat Kala Bhavan, Varanasi.

*akāro viṣṇurūddista aukārastu maheśvaraḥ*
*makārehoocyate brahmā praṇavena trayo matāḥ.*

*Oṁ*, the cosmic (*primal*) sound is, *a*, *au*, *ma*, that represent three phases of the cosmic cycle — creation (Brahmā), preservation (Viṣṇu) and dissolution (Śiva) — condensed into a single sound unit.

*Yājñavalkya Smṛti (Śabda-Kalpadruma, Prathama Bhāga)*

*uṁtye tadakṣaramidam sarvam*
*tasyopāvyākhyānaṁ bhūtam bhaveta*
*bhaviṣyaditi sarvamoṁkāra evam*
*yachhanyata trikālatītam tadapyonkara*

The Primal sound is the basis of cosmic evolution.

(*Māṇḍūkyopaniṣad*)

10. *Erotic Sculpture* — Koṇārka, *ca.* 11th century AD.

11. *Kalyāṇa Sunder* (Marriage of Śiva and Pārvatī) — Stone, Pratihāra school, *ca.* 10th century AD, Prov. Etāh (U.P.), Bharat Kala Bhavan, Varanasi.

In *pāṇigrahaṇa*, i.e., during Śiva's marriage with Pārvatī, he appears in his *saumya* aspect. The divine marriage is said to have been witnessed by gods and goddesses. The marriage not only signifies the divine union but also signifies the unity among the different deities. Where he is with Pārvatī, they signify the unity of *Puruṣa* and *Prakṛti* or of spirit and matter or the unity of essence and substance.

12. *Bhairava* — Bharat Kala Bhavan, Varanasi.

Bhairava refers to the form of Śiva inspiring dread and terror. In this form he overcomes Time (*kāla*) and becomes one transcending time (*mahākāla*). He is terrific (*bhīṣaṇa*) and he sustains (*bharaṇa*) — hence known as Bhairava.

13. *Viśvarūpa Viṣṇu*— Rāma's mystical appearance before Kauśalyā, Jaipur substyle. *ca.* AD 1815, Bharat Kala Bhavan, Varanasi.

14. *Hanu-Bhairava* — (Wall Painting), Bhairava Temple, Varanasi.

15. *Dancing Gaṇeśa* — Stone, Pratihāra School, *ca.* 9th century AD, Prov. Kannauj, Bharat Kala Bhavan, Varanasi.

16. *Celestial Woman with Flowers* — Bharat Kala Bhavan, Varanasi.

17. *Cakra-Puruṣa* — Nepali Scroll, Bharat Kala Bhavan, Varanasi.

18. *Hairuka* — Bharat Kala Bhavan, Varanasi.

19. *Mañjuśrī* — Bharat Kala Bhavan, Varanasi.

20. *Cakra, Maṇḍala and Trikoṇa* — Nepali Scroll, Bharat Kala Bhavan, Varanasi.

21. (A & B) *Cakra (Wheel)* — Sun temple Koṇārka, *ca.* 11th century AD.

*Cakra* is the symbol of universe. There is an explanation, based primarily on the philosophical concepts of *Upaniṣad*, according to which the function of *cakra* can be defined as the principle of life and energy.

22. *Śiva-Temple* — Udayeśvara, Madhya Pradesh, about 11th century AD.

23. *Kandarīya Mahādeva*—Khajurāho, Madhya Pradesh, *ca.* 10th century AD.

    There is a *tīrtha* where one should always bath and this is the *tīrtha* of the mind (*mānasatīrtha*). Its water is truth (*satya*), that is deep, clear and pure. So the temple should be built where *tīrtha* is.

24. *Śata-dala-Kamala* — National Museum, New Delhi.

25. *Buddha* — Stone, *ca.* 5th century AD, Site Museum, Sarnath, Varanasi.

26. *Alasa Kanyā* — Stone, Chandela Period, *ca.* 11th century AD, Prov. Khajurāho, Bharat Kala Bhavan.

27. *Liṅga-Yoni*— (Kāśī Viśvanāth a Temple), Varanasi.

28. *Sun* — Dacani School, *ca.* 18th century AD, Private Collection.

# 1

# Introduction

THE principles of *Tantra* were conceived by great minds with the best of intentions. But unfortunately, in course of time, its principles came in for severe criticism and were often decried as ridiculous and detestable. It appears that such conclusions may have been made due to misconceptions about the subject. For one, the mysteries and the esoteric elements in *Tantra* were neither properly understood nor, where well understood, considered in their right perspective. The mysteries and speculations attached to the concept were also not explained to the desired extent. As a result, the subject remained the preserve of a small group of initiated persons and attempts were never undertaken to popularise the essence of Tāntric religion among the common people.

However, some scholars tried to enter into the mysteries of *Tantra* and they traced the basic principles of *Tantra* — the nucleus of it, so to say — in the Mother Goddess cult of the proto-historic Indus Valley Civilization. Subsequently, the Ṛgvedic *Devī Sūkta* discussing the mysteries of Brahmā and Vāc, the speculations in *Atharvaveda*, the *Brahma-māyā* of *Upaniṣad*, the concept of *Puruṣa-Prakṛti* of *Sāṁkhya* Philosophy, Purāṇic mother goddesses (Aṁbikā, Bhavānī, Bhadrakālī, Durgā, Umā-Maheśvarī) offered the required momentum and solid foundations to the concept of the *Tantra*. The philosophy and the religion of

*Tantra* was thus formulated and in course of time it made a tremendous impact on the medieval religions *viz*., Brāhmaṇical Hinduism, Buddhism and Jainism. The impact of Tāntric tenets also seeped into the medieval paintings and sculptural art of India. The influence of Tāntric religion and philosophy is found recorded in the religious texts. The *Śaiva-āgama* literature, the *Vaiṣṇava āgamas* like *Pañcarātra* and *Vaikhānasa* and much of *Śākta* literature laid bare the notions of Tāntric religion and philosophy. Similarly, texts like *Mañjuśrīmūlakalpa, Saddharmapuṇḍarīka, Prajñāpāramitā, Sādhanamālā, Niṣpanna Yogāvalī* and some other texts incorporated different notions and rituals of *Tantra* in Buddhist religion, philosophy and iconography.

The earlier concept of Buddhism lost itself significantly in the maze of Tāntric mysticism and esotericism, and it was practically overwhelmed by the introduction of host of *mudrās*, *maṇḍalas*, *kriyās* and *caryās*. Buddhism now began to incorporate elements like magical spells, exorcism, recognition of demons and female deities (Śakti), and at the same time, yoga and sexoyogic practices. All these resulted in a significant change and what emerged came to be called Tāntric Buddhism. Likewise, significant changes were noticed in the concept of Brāhmaṇical Hinduism. Hindus, under the spell of *Tantra*, concentrated on *jñāna* (philosophical doctrines), *yoga* (meditation), *kriyā* (activities such as idol-making, temple building), and *caryā* (observances). They started paying attention to *mantras* (prayers), *bījas* (mystic syllables), *yantras* (diagrams) and *nyāsas* (identifying deities in different parts of the body of the devotee). Tāntrism did not spare Jainism even. The cult of mother goddess, magical rites, the efficacy of *mantras* and spells, incantations, etc. that were accorded recognition in the Jain pantheon, were, in fact, imbibed from Tāntrism. However, the spell of Tāntrism could not significantly affect the Jain religion and it continued with certain rigid rules and prescriptions of its own.

Any understanding of the Tāntric religion would require a recognition of some of its essential characteristics.

The Tāntric religion gives supreme importance to the body (*deha* or *kāyā*) and it categorically admits that the mysteries of the universe may be sought in the body itself. Of the two aspects of Tāntrism, *viz.*, the sophisticated and the popular, the former incorporates a number of Brāhmaṇical Hindu elements — one of which is the concept of Śakti. Śakti resides in human body as the serpent power (*kuṇḍalinī*) within *mulādhāra cakra*. The dormant female energy is awakened by yogic exercises and then she is to be taken up through the regions of five other *cakras* to the realm of *sahasrāra*. If a *sādhaka* gets success in this nearly impossible endeavour, he attains salvation and the highest virtues. The term *mantra* includes two powers *viz.*, the *vācaka* and *vācya*. The word *vācaka* embodies words as well as sounds. There are two grades of sound and these are called *bindu* and *nāda*. *Bindu* is Śiva, *bīja* is Śakti, while the term *nāda* combines Śiva and Śakti. Śiva is recognised as the male principle and Śakti denotes the female principle, and through their union (*kāma-kalā*) proceeds creation (*śṛṣṭi*). Śiva is passive, Śakti is active and without Śakti, Śiva is rendered into *śava* (corpse).

A brief discussion of some aspects of Hindu thought and of the Indian philosophical tradition, with reference to the mystical in it, in what follows would provide a background-of-sorts to understanding the Tāntric view of things.

Throughout the history of the Hindu civilization there has been a certain inspiring ideal, a certain motive power, a certain way of looking at life, which cannot be identified with any one stage of the process. Hinduism has grown not by accretion, but like an organism, undergoing from time to time transformation as a whole. It has carried within it much of its early attributes. It is the historic vitality, the abounding energy that it reveals, which alone is evidence of its spiritual genius. The unity of Hinduism is not one of an unchanging creed or a fixed deposit of doctrine, but is the unity of a continuously changing life. The religion is an experience and an attitude of the mind, a consciousness of the ultimate reality and not a theory about God. The religious genius is a prophet, sage or a *ṛṣi* who embodies in himself the spiritual vision. When the soul goes inward into itself it draws near its own divine root and becomes pervaded by the radiance of another nature. The aim of all religions is the realization of the highest truth. It is the intuition of reality (*brahmānubhava*), insight into truth (*brahmāṇdarasanā*), contact with the supreme (*brahmānśansparśa*), direct apprehension of reality (*brahmanśasākṣātkāra*), that form the basic elements of Hindu philosophy.

If religion is experience what is that we experience? What is the nature of reality? The object which hunts the human soul as a presence is at once all-embracing and infinite, and is envisaged in many different ways. The Vedic people recognised the higher concepts of gods like the Sky and the Mother Earth, the Sun and the Fire. The reality as they experienced it cannot be fully expressed though it defies all description. Individuality, whether human or divine, can only be accepted as a given fact and cannot be described. Our thinking is controlled by something beyond itself which is perception in the physical sciences and the intuition of God in the science of religion. *The Kena Upaniṣad* says, 'The eye does not go there, nor speech nor mind.We do not know that. We do not understand how one can teach it? It is different from the known, it is also above the unknown' (1.2-4). The *Bhāṣya* on *Brahma Sūtra* (III.2.7) of Śaṅkara quotes a Vedic passage where the teacher tells the pupils the secret of the self by keeping silent about it. 'Really, I tell you, but you understand not, the self is silence'. The *ṛṣi* says that wonderful is the man that can speak him, and wonderful is also the man that can understand him (*Kaṭha Upaniṣad*, 1.2.7). The eternal being is beyond all personal limitations, though the sustainer of all forms is still beyond them. Religion arises out of the experiences of the human spirit which feels its kinship and continuity with the Divine. Worship is the acknowledgement of the magnificence of this supreme reality. From beginning, attempts have been made to bring God (the supreme being) closer to the needs of man.

The Indian philosophical tradition has been a quest, both of an immediate experience of reality and of an achievement of the good and just life. Men and society have been nourished in India not by ethical and social, but by mystical and trans-social doctrines and ideals. Metaphysics thus becomes the law of man's social living. The Indian ethical system is built on the foundation of metaphysics, certain doctrines and symbols, and all these invest morality with rich, trans-human meanings. Metaphysics and religion both impart superhuman meanings to the evolutionary process and encourage mankind to evaluate, order and direct it as frequently as it suffers defeat at the hands of nature. Whosoever feels a universal love for his fellow creatures will rejoice in conferring bliss on them, and thus attaining *nirvāṇa* on the basis of his apprehension of non-duality, he overcomes ignorance and sorrow, secures peace, and never suffers degradation. Man reaches his highest moral stature when his feelings, joy and reverence reflect themselves in his relations to the external world through a more sensitive, universalized conscience in terms of complete acceptance, peace and an all-transcending compassion or love. Such is the indispensable contribution of the mystical consciousness to the elevation of moral standards through the discipline of human nature for progress.

One of my chief intentions in writing this book is to show the Indian conception of the relevance of philosophy to life — an understanding that should not remain merely in theory but needs to be adopted to mould our entire personality, drive us through spiritual strife on the onward path of self-realization and make us share the duties of social life in the best manner conceivable.

# 2

# Religious Mythology

ALTHOUGH Ṛgvedic mythology is not as primitive as some scholars once believed it to be, in no other literary monument of the world do we come across this primitive phase of the evolution of religious beliefs which reveals to us the very process of personification by which natural phenomena came to be conceived as gods. The name of the god often hides but little.

In the Ṛgvedic hymns to the Dawn, the Sun and the Fire (Agni), among others, the corresponding physical phenomena is mentioned as diectly exercising its beneficent powers. The process of personification made a gradual progress, in that the personified phenomenon was deified, and thus the concrete figures of Sūrya and Agni emerged. The gods are benevolent, the only one with malevolent traits being Rudra. Rudra is a subordinate deity in the *Ṛgveda.* He has braided hair, a brown-complexion and a glorious necklace (*niśka*). He is the father of Maruts. He is fierce like a terrible beast and is called a bull as well as the ruddy boar of heaven. He is exalted as the mightiest of the mighty. He is the lord (*Iśāna*) and father of the world. He is easily invoked and is auspicious (Śiva). He is the great physician. It is suggested that the storm in its destructive aspect may explain the malevolent side of his nature. The conception of Rudra-Śiva in the *Atharvaveda* actually represents a transitional state between the conception of Rudra in *Ṛgveda* and the systematic philosophy of Śaivism in *Śvetāsvatara Upaniṣad*. On the whole, a very optimistic outlook on life is revealed in the hymns of the *Ṛgveda*. The Ṛgvedic people were much involved with the joys and pleasures of this world. There is no trace of pessimism in the thoughts of the Ṛgvedic people.

The evolution of religion and philosophical thought in the post-Ṛgvedic age begins with the *Atharvaveda* which has preserved an aspect of the primitive religious ideas which is not to be found in the other Vedic texts. It must be admitted that the religion of the *Atharvaveda*, being more popular than priestly, formed a transitional stage to the idolatry and superstitions of the ignorant masses rather than to the sublimated pantheism of the *Upaniṣad*, and further that it led to magic being confused with mysticism.

In the *Sāmaveda* and *Yajurveda* the concept of sacrifice dominates everything. A very large number of the songs and spells of *Atharvaveda* naturally fit in, most admirably, into the framework of the domestic rites, as a substantial part of them partook of the nature of magic rites. The sacrifices, which could bend even the gods to the will of the sacrificer, became the only power of significance and old gods were not of much consequence now. As a result, some of the minor deities of *Ṛgveda* disappeared or existed in name only.

Snake-worship (borrowed from the aborigines) and motifs made their appearance now, and Viṣṇu was accorded a high position among the deities. Desire was seen as the germ of existence — the motive power of all creation. The starting point of creation was either the primeval waters or the non-existent or the *Brahman*. Man was born with certain *ṛṇas* or debts which he had to discharge in his life. He discharged these debts, if he worshipped the gods, performed funeral ceremonies and offered oblations to the *bhūtas*. Truthfulness in utterance and action was the foundation of moral life.

It is also necessary to make a few general observations on certain important aspects of Vedic religion. It is not possible to accept the view that all worship of the gods is to be traced to the cult of the dead. The human worshipper, realizing his weakness and utter helplessness, leant, as it were, for support on the powerful gods. Magic and religion are never confused in the Vedic religion.

It may be concluded from the above discussion that religious thought during the period does not present a very consistent picture. However, a central idea was becoming clear from the mass of incoherent urges which went under the generic name of *dharma*. These bonds were further strengthened by the singing in sacred chants, worshipping gods in quest of higher things and a continual research for the Absolute. The intellectual fervour expressed itself in the *Upaniṣads*. These aspirations moulded values, ideas and forms of discipline through religious teachings and a well-regulated system of education. The discipline implied a double process, the relinquishment of the greed for life and growth of the personal self into the universal self. The end of this discipline was variously named — self-realisation (*siddhi*), emancipation (*mukti*), enlightenment (*jñāna*), freedom (*nirvāṇa*), bliss (*ānanda*). In substance, it was the absolute integration of human personality (*kaivalya*) freed from the limitations of attachment and fear. The quest of the Absolute became predominant in Indian culture. The Absolute descended on earth in human form; the aspirant, by absolute surrender, attained him.

The Vedic religion lost credit and a twofold reaction ensued — an atheistic movement which frankly denied the necessity, if not also the reality, of the Vedic gods together with the pre-eminence of the brāhmaṇas in spiritual matters and a monotheistic movement which accepted devotion (*bhakti*) as the only way of pleasing and attaining a personal God.

The seventh century and onwards was marked by waves of intense activity in many lands where man had emerged from the Bronze Age. In India, where a highly complex civilization had been flourishing for centuries, religious life in the period, 750-320 BC displayed some characteristic features. The first and foremost was the prevalence of the images of gods, as worship and meditation of the Supreme Being was thought possible only when he was endowed with form. There was the belief that the form of the Supreme Being, as He manifests Himself, should be worshipped according to the rites prescribed. Another characteristic feature was the spirit of toleration among the followers of different religious sects. One aspect of this tolerant spirit was the attempt to establish the unity of different gods. The very idea of the Trinity of Brahmā, Viṣṇu and Śiva is an evidence of the same spirit, which is further displayed in that the Buddha came to be regarded as an incarnation of Viṣṇu.

This period was lit up by the personality of two great reformers, Mahāvīra and Gautam Buddha. They were wandering ascetics who ignored God and denied the *Vedas*, and revolted against the superiority of the brāhmaṇas. There were people who attacked the Vedic religion and discarded the *Vedas* completely and openly. One such person was Cārvaka. But the more powerful, systematic and philosophic attacks were led by the founders of Jainism and Buddhism. *Sāṁkhya* and *Upaniṣads* were the sources of their inspiration; the gospel of freedom from misery and even the theory of *karma* (action) were borrowed by them from contemporary religious thought and merely systematised.

The religious sects, Śaivism, Vaiṣṇavism, Jainism and Buddhism, played an important part in the subsequent history. All of them had as their common ground, the repudiation, explicit or implied, of the Brāhmaṇical claim that the *Vedas* were the infallible source of spiritual truth, and the rituals prescribed therein the sole means of salvation or emancipation. But there was also a fundamental difference among them. While the first two were theistic and centred round two Vedic deities Śiva and Viṣṇu, the last two did not recognise the Vedic gods, or for that matter, any god at all.

The essential elements common between the two theistic religions, Śaivism and Vaiṣṇavism, are *bhakti* (devotion) and *prasāda* (divine grace). The former means intense love and devotion of the worshipper to his beloved god, even to the extent of complete self-surrender. The latter means the grace of God which brings salvation to the devotee. Jainism and Buddhism had also many elements in common. Philosophically, they both started from the same fundamental principle that the world is full of misery, and the object of religion is to find means of deliverance from the endless cycle of births and deaths which bring men repeatedly into this world. As *karma* (action), or an individual's actions, is the root-cause of rebirth, emphasis is laid upon conduct and the practice of austerities in varying degrees of severity as the chief means of salvation, rather than on sacrifice or prayers to the personal god. Jainism and Buddhism both imply a system of philosophy and social organization, with a code of morality and cult of their own, which together gave to their followers a sense of religious solidarity. Both are inspired by the ascetic ideals and the philosophy of the *Upaniṣads*.

In the field of philosophical ideas, the heterodox religions showed a number of features suggestive of either a borrowing from, or a survival of, the thought-currents of the primitive peoples. There are some features common to Jainism and Buddhism and the *Sāṁkhya* (yoga) philosophy, which go back to the primitive currents of religious and philosophical speculation. To the same primitive influence must also be attributed another important feature in the development of religions during this period, *viz.*, the introduction of image worship. In assessing the truth, it should be borne in mind that Vedic literature is almost exclusively concerned with beliefs and practices. The aboriginal inhabitants are scornfully referred to as worshippers of the phallic emblem — later associated with Śiva. In the *Upaniṣads*, we find an important distinction drawn between *aparā* (lower knowledge) and *parā* (higher knowledge)[1] and between *avidyā* and *vidyā* (false and true knowledge).[2] The voluminous Vedic literature, with all its auxiliaries and ceremonies, was gradually losing its importance in the eye of thinking men. It is then that philosophic minds turned towards enlightenment, and the distinction between *karma* (work) and *jñāna* (meditation) — where a higher value was assigned to meditation — was introduced. In the post-Vedic period, however, rituals permeated the Indian mind to such an extent that it was almost impossible to separate religion from ritualistic worship and mystical utterances (*mantra*).

The Śākta cult, that evolved with the concept of the female principle, is next in importance to the two major cults of the *Vaiṣṇava* and *Śaiva*. Perhaps, Śakti was identified with the tongues of Agni (fire) and named accordingly. Her destructive aspect gave her such names as Kālī (the destroyer), Karālī (the terrible), Bhīmā (the frightful), Caṇḍī, Caṇḍikā or Cāmuṇḍā (the wrathful) and she was also identified with Sarasvatī and Vāk (speech). In the *Brāhmaṇa* literature, *vāk* or speech is depicted as a source of strength. Naturally, the Goddess (Devī) *par excellence* became a source of power and Sarasvatī, the goddess of learning, came to be recognised as the revealer of divine wisdom. Association with some abstract qualities and virtues personified also enhanced her prestige. Some factors that invested the Devī with power had their origin in philosophy. The *Sāṁkhya* philosophy had familiarised the idea that *puruṣa* is by nature inactive and it is *prakṛti* who is active. The *Vedānta* system in its *advaita* form could claim an Upaniṣadic origin for its conception that the *brahman* becomes the creator only when associated with *māyā*, which was subsequently called the function of *brahman*. Atheistic sects hastened to add that *māyā* was none other than *prakṛti* while the *māyin* was Maheśvara.

Now *māyā* in its alternative meanings signified both *prajñā* (insight) and *svapna* (illusion/dream) and it was deified as Sarasvatī and Moharātri. Hence power, wisdom and the stupefying capacity were added to the creative agency to make the composite picture of a goddess who as Mahālakṣmī (called Śakti in Tāntric literature) created even the gods and as Yoganidrā sent all creation to sleep. The primal energy (*ādyā śakti*) appears as Mahālakṣmī. The Devī was also manifest as the motivating energy and was known as the 'Divine Mother'. She was regarded as capable of absorbing all the forms and resuming her unitary character as the Supreme Goddess from whom all creation, preservation and destruction proceeded. It is difficult to say to what extent the pre-Vedic culture of India contributed to the conception of a mother goddess of the type now familiar to us as Śakti.

A relationship was established between Śaivism and Śāktism and assimilation of the two creeds was rapid. The one noticeable aspect about the Śiva-Śakti cult, that both Śiva and Śakti were worshipped in benign as well as terrible forms, helped an easy alliance between the two. This led to the emergence and development of the *Tantra* cult, which profoundly influenced Śaivism, Vaiṣṇavism and Buddhism, and radically changed their views and practices.

Śaivism attained a dominant position in India during the period under review in the material manifestation of religious fervour. But there was also a parallel philosophical movement which tended to fix the tenets of Śaivism. While the main principles remained the same, there were the local variants, and so we have schools ranging from pluralistic realism to monistic idealism. There is a form of Śaivism, popularly known as Kāśmīr Śaivism. The system known as *trika*, *spanda* and *pratyabhijñā*, the triple principle with which the system deals being Siva, Śakti *Aṇu*, or *Pati-Pāśa-Paśu*, is acceptable to many schools of Śaivism. Kāśmīr Śaivism regards the individual soul and the world as essentially identical with Śiva, and so the three, according to it, are reducible to one. The term *spanda* indicates the principle of apparent movement or change from the state of absolute unity to the plurality of the world and the expression *pratyabhijñā* which means 'recognition' refers to the way of realising the soul's identity with Śiva. The Ultimate Reality, in every school of *Śaiva* philosophy, is Śaṁbhu or Śiva, the Supreme God. Śiva is the *ātman*, the self of all beings, immutable and ever perfect. He is pure consciousness (*caitanya*), absolute experience (*parā saṁvit*), Supreme Lord (*parameśvara*). He is the ground of all existence, substrate of all beings. He is without any beginning or end. He resides in all that moves and that which moves not as well. Time and space do not limit Him, for He transcends them, and they are but His appearance. He is both immanent (*viśvamāyā*) and transcendent (*viśvotīrṇa*). The world does not exhaust Him, for He is infinite. He is called *anuttara*, the reality beyond which there is nothing. The Ultimate Reality is beyond the reach of thought and language. Yet mind and speech attempt to understand and express the Real in its relation to the Universe.

The pure consciousness which is the Supreme Reality and is referred to as Śiva is the material as well as the efficient cause of the universe. This view is much the same as the one sponsored by *Advaita-Vedānta* regarding the *Saguṇa Brahman*. God or Reality is the substance of which the world is made as well as the instrument which makes it. Fundamentally, there is no difference between the cause and the effect. But while for *advaita* the manifested world is non-real, for Kāśmīra Śaivism it is real.

The manifestation of the universe is effected through the power (Śakti) of Śiva. And power is not different from the possessor thereof. Śakti is the creative energy of Śiva and is spoken of as His feminine aspect. There are innumerable modes of Śakti, but most important of them are five. They are — *cit śakti*, the power of intelligence or self-luminosity, which means that the

Supreme shines by itself without dependence on any other light and even in the absence of all objects; *ānanda śakti*, the power of independence (*svātantrya*) which is bliss or joy, and by virtue of which the Ultimate Reality is self-satisfied; *icchā-śakti*, the power of will or desire, the wonderful power of the Lord to create; *jñāna śakti*, the power of knowledge by virtue of which the objects are brought together and held together in consciousness; and *kriyā śakti*, the power of action which is responsible for the actual manifestation of objects and their relations. By these powers the Supreme Śiva in His aspects as Śakti has manifested Himself as the Universe. He has manifested Himself by His own free will (*svecchayā*) and in Himself as the substratum. That is, there is nothing other than Śiva. If the universe appears (as if) different, such appearance is a delusion. With the opening out of Śakti, the universe appears; and when Śakti closes herself up, the universe disappears, *sṛṣṭi* (creation) and *pralaya* (dissolution) alternate; and this process is without any beginning or end.

Śiva, the Ultimate Reality, holds the potentiality of creation. The reality is that the universe is an appearance. The *śivatattva* is the first stage in the process of world manifestation. Of the five aspects of Śakti, *cit* or intelligence predominates over the others at this stage. The next category or *tattva* is Śakti. It is not proper to call it *ānanda śakti*, for it is by virtue of its operation that the manifestation of the *śivatattva* is made possible. When Śakti is counted separately, what is meant in reality is the manifestation of its *ānanda* aspect — the aspect of bliss and self-satisfaction which is the precursor of the manifestation of a variety of forms. Salvation consists in the soul's recognition of its identity with the Ultimate Reality. As bondage is the result of ignorance, release is to be attained through knowledge (the spiritual intuition of the fundamental unity) which liberates.

Mere human efforts will not be of much avail in the path to *mokṣa*. What really matters here is the Divine Will. Besides the powers of creation, preservation and destruction of the universe,

God has the powers of conceal and grace. His real nature is concealed from the soul; and after the soul has played out its part in the world (*saṁsāra*), God's grace descends on the individual and the individual is released. The descent of Divine Gracc is called *śakti nipāta. Mokṣa* is a return to the original state of perfection and purity of consciousness, a release from the cycles of death and birth. The released soul is merged in *brahman*, the elements having been resolved into the substance of Śiva, and no grief or delusion can befall him who surveys the universe as *brahman*. There is no duality between the soul and God (Śiva), each qualified by Śakti, and God and soul are in an inseparable union through the inalienable power called Śakti but the individual soul is neither absolutely identical with, nor entirely different from, God. It is a part of which God is the whole; it is the body of which God is the soul. It enjoys the bliss of Śiva (*sālokya*) — what is known as the mystic union of soul with Śiva (*sāmīpya*) and experiences unity-in-duality (*sārūpya*).

Parāśiva is the supreme reality, the One or the Absolute without a second. He is of the nature of existence (*sat*), consciousness (*cit*) and bliss (*ānanda*). He is the Supreme Power, Omniscient, most glorious, and endowed with all auspicious qualities. The universe of souls and matter is but a part of him, a projection of His will. The manifestation of the universe, however, does not affect Him in any way. He himself does not undergo any change or diminution. Śiva is the material and the instrumental cause of the universe. He is immanent as well as transcendent. From him all beings spring into existence; in Him they live; and unto Him they return at the end. Without beginning, middle or end, He is the one all-pervading Reality, of the nature of consciousness and bliss, without form wonderful. United with Umā, the Parameśvara is the Lord with three eyes (*trinetra*) and a blue-throat (*nīlakaṇṭha*), and is quiescent.

Śakti is the power which eternally resides in Paramaśiva as His inseparable attribute. It is the ultimate creative principle, *mūla-prakṛti* or *māyā*, which evolves itself into the phenomenal universe. The *māyā* in Vīraśaivism is not to be understood in the sense of principles of illusion of *Advaita Vedānta*. The word means 'that which naturally attains to and eternally resides' in the supreme *Brahman*. As heat is to fire and light to Sun, Śakti is to Śiva, inseparably united with Him as His attribute. It is through his Śakti that Śiva becomes the cause of the universe. Śiva lends His own nature to Śakti, and in its discriminative or differentiating aspect (*vimarśakhya*), it becomes the agent of world-manifestation. Out of Śakti come all beings that constitute the universe. This is called creation (*sṛṣṭi*). And in *pralaya* (destruction) all return to Śakti and remain there in the form of seeds.

The individual soul (*jīva*) is a part (*aṅśa*) of Śiva, and it imagines itself to be different from Him on account of ignorance (*avidyā*). The soul is identical with Śiva in the sense that it proceeds from Śiva, partakes of His essence, and finds ultimate rest in Him. Having no independent existence, it finally becomes one with Him on the removal of ignorance. It is also distinct from Śiva in the sense that though sharing in His essence, it does not possess the attributes of omniscience, omnipotence, etc. It is a victim of impurities such as *karma* and *māyā*, and is consequently a creature of *saṁsāra*. The final goal of the soul is conceived as *aikya* or unity with Parāśiva, the Supreme Reality. The soul in union with Śiva enjoys unexcelled bliss. This final state of experience is called *liṅgāṅga sāmarasya* — essence between *liṅga* (Śiva) and *aṅga* (soul = *ātman*). *Liṅga* is Śiva or Rudra, and is the object of worship or adoration. *Aṅga*, which means part, is the individual soul and is the worshipper or adorer. Sakti also gets divided into two parts — *kalā* and *bhakti*, the former referring to Śiva and the latter to the individual soul. *Kalā* is responsible for the projection of the world from Śiva. *Bhakti* leads the soul from bondage to final release. Śiva is *sat* and *cit*. As *sat*, Śiva is the plenitude of being and incomprehensible. As *cit* or consciousness, we can know him. Śiva as *nirguṇa* means that he is above the three attributes (*guṇa*) of *prakṛti* (*sattva*, *raja* and *tama*). Śiva is of the form of the universe (*viśvarūpa*) and exceeds the world. His greatness is beyond conception, and is neither the object of perception nor the content of thought. Śiva is the male, female, neuter and yet none of these. Śiva or Rudra is *viśvādhika* (more than the universe), the cosmological argument to establish the efficient causality of Śiva in relation to the world. The universe is subject to the states of origin (*sṛṣṭi*), substance (*sthiti*) and destruction (*saṁhāra* or *pralaya*), concealment (*tirobhāva* or *tirodhāna*) and bestowal of grace (*anugraha*). The first four have the last as their goal.

## References

1. *Muṇḍaka Upaniṣad*, 1.4.
2. *Kaṭha Upaniṣad*, 1.2.5.

# 3

# The Concept of the Tantra

THE word *'Tantra'* has been derived from the root *tan* (to spread) with the suffix *strāna* added. Some have traced it to the root *tatrī* or *tantrī* (to originate or to know), while two roots *tan* and *tantrī* have elsewhere been identified and used in the sense of spreading or weaving. In its present and widely-accepted sense, *Tantra* means a body of literature which spreads knowledge, particularly knowledge of profound things with the aid of mystic diagrams (*yantra*) and words possessing esoteric meanings (*mantra*), and helps in the attainment of salvation. As a matter of fact, however, the term *'Tantra'* has been used in different ways: it is used in an ordinary non-religious sense in different philosophical systems, and it is only in later literature, from about fifth or sixth century AD, that *Tantra* as a special religious or philosophical concept comes into use. The earliest uses of the word *'Tantra'* found in the *Srauta-Sūtras*, the *Harivaṁśa*, *Suśruta*, the *Sāṁkhya* philosophy and didactic fables do not bear the meaning of a special literature dedicated to the cult of Śakti. The images of the Mother are referred to in the *Bṛhat-Saṁhitā*. But neither Amara in his *Amarakośa* nor Bāṇabhaṭṭa in his works refers to the followers of Śakti, though both were familiar with the Divine Mother concept and Amara was certain of the power (*śakti*) of *mantras*.

It is necessary at this stage to issue a note of warning. Though

Śāktism and *Tantra* are now so much identified that the word '*Tantra*' is almost reserved for the religious literature of the *Śāktas*, the term *Āgama* is confined to the *Śaiva*s and *Saṁhitā* and *Rātra* (knowledge) to the *Vaiṣṇava*s, the earlier use of the word '*Tantra*' was quite flexible and it could be applied to the *Vaiṣṇava* and the *Śaiva* sacred literature as well. The division of Brāhmaṇical religious literature was into *Veda, Smṛti, Purāṇa* and *Tantra*, arranged in the chronological order and assigned to the four ages of the world. The justification for this is that it is only after the *Purāṇa* had established the pre-eminence of Viṣṇu, Śiva and Śakti, that the *Tantra* could get underway. It does not mean, however, that these divisions had nothing in common among them.

The antiquity of the term '*Tantra*' in the now-accepted sense is difficult to determine. The origin of the *Tāntrika* cult and the composition of texts may be older. We get a fair idea of the general principles of Tāntric belief from the *Mahānirvāṇa Tantra* which, though of later date, is one of the most popular and well-known Tāntric texts. Almost like a Vedāntic text, it deals with *Brahman*, which according to the *Śākta*s is nothing but Śakti, the eternal dynamic source of all beings. It is perceived that all life proceeds from the womb of woman; so we should think of the ultimate creative principle in terms of the 'mother' and not of the 'father'. Philosophical concepts like *prakṛti* and *māyā*, and mythological figures like Pārvatī, Durgā, Lakṣmī and Rādhā constitute the female principle of creation and are merely different names of the female principle of the Mother of the world. This sect, therefore, looks upon every woman as an incarnation of the Universal Mother and as one to whom proper respect should be paid.

The *Tantra*, as a matter of fact, became equally popular with the higher castes and classes as well as with the lower castes. And this form of worship was open to women also. Perhaps no religious literature of India has raised such controversy on evaluation as the *Tantra*. On the one hand, they have been extolled as the repository of sublime truth, rigorous discipline, catholic outlook and as an indispensable means to the attainment of the highest spirituality. On the other hand, they have been seen as a type of composition containing meaningless jargon, mysterious mummery, obscenity, and revolting antinomianism. We have, in fact, a strange mixture of higher and lower thoughts: theurgy and thaumaturgy jostle with high philosophy and deep devotion, dark rites and liberal thoughts go cheek by jowl with one another, and accurate knowledge alternates with the occult. The presence of strenuous discipline as well as moral laxity, of sound understanding and primitive credulity yields a chequered pattern, bewilders the curious enquirer and confuses the novice in practice. The matter is further complicated by the fact that the language used is sometimes enigmatical, and has both an exoteric and an esoteric meaning. Thus, without the help of an adept (interpreter), the proper sense is likely to be missed. Hence *dīkṣā* (initiation) by a teacher (*guru*) is essential for getting access to the esoteric or real meaning of a particular word or sentence, a meaning handed down traditionally in different Tāntric schools and not communicated to those who did not join the particular fraternity. It is the teacher who opens the eyes of his disciple to the true meaning and guides him through the dark to the realm of light which is the spiritual kingdom.

It is obvious that such a complicated system, in which the lower and the higher elements of human nature tussle with one another, could not have been a matter of sudden growth; nor could it have been derived from a single source, particularly if we consider the complexity of its practices and the diversity of the creed involved. On *a priori* grounds it may even be surmised that systematization must have been preceded by popular beliefs and rites connected with the worship of the various female deities, of which the cult of the Mother became the most prominent. The dark forces of nature embodied man's fear of the mysterious and the terrifying without and within, and his hope that they could be pacified and controlled by appropriate incantations, sacrifices and meditations. That they appealed to something universal in man in his primitive thinking is attested to by the presence of similar beliefs in many other cultures in other parts of the globe. That Brāhmaṇism, Jainism and Buddhism should all develop or incorporate occultism, in course of time, and fall back upon the use of magic syllables (*mantra*) and mystic diagrams (*yantra*) shows that they had to take note of the basic needs of the human mind in a composite population drawn from different social and cultural strata, and diverse tribal and racial strains. The different components of *Tantra* owed their existence to these diverse needs and emphasised them as they developed in space and time.

The use of five *makāras* [*madirā* (wine), *matsya* (fish), *māṁsa* (meat), *mudrā* (parched grain) and *maithuna* (coition)] could be made under certain prescribed conditions of discipline without secrecy in appropriate places and times. It was intended to further the progress of the aspirant towards the elimination of all empirical distinctions and the attainment of complete freedom. The *Kulārṇava Tantra* tells us that just as one rises with the help of the very ground on which one has fallen, so also it is through drinking life to the very lees that one has to make the spiritual ascent. A thorn has to be eradicated with the help of another thorn; similarly, indulgence must be forced to yield satiety and higher value. Wine which merely intoxicates is a sinful beverage, but as the producer of a euphoric condition, in which care and anxiety are absent, it is a desirable drink. Similarly, flesh that nourishes the body, fish that increases sexual potency, grain that invigorates the system, and coition that brings about a blissful condition (*mahāsukha*) and prolongs the race at the same time, are all intended to keep the practitioner in a fit condition of body and mind to pursue spiritual aims. It is obvious that in some cases, these failed to serve their legitimate purpose, especially when promiscuity was permitted with different types of women, mostly coming from lower castes and dubbed as Śakti. There was, however, a general prohibition against using any women except one's wife for the purpose of the last of the five *tattva* (*maithuna*), and there were also other restrictions. The idea was that a practitioner must go beyond dualities of all kinds of love and hate, merit and demerit such as touchable and untouchable, forbidden and non-forbidden, or delectable and nauseating in food and drink, and prohibited and non-prohibited in sex relations, male and female, friend and foe, etc. to cultivate not only equanimity in himself but also equality towards all.

It is only when this state of mind is acquired that the last stage of sanctification is reached, namely *kaulācāra*. This is the *divya* (superior) condition, for then the aspirant transcends the likings and dislikings of earthly life. To God all things are equal. Pity and cruelty are equally devoid of meaning in the ultimate reference, and so also is approbated and unapprobated conduct. Just as one of the *Upaniṣads* has said that, to one who has attained the knowledge of the *brahman* no sin can be attached for any kind of antinomian act, so also the *Tantra* places the *Kaula* (worshipper of *Kula* or *Śakti*) above all moral judgements and puts no prohibitions and restraints in his way, viewing them as unnecessary for one who has pierced the veil of space and time, process and differentiation. A *kaula* practices all rituals at will, being at heart a *Śākta*, outwardly a *Śaiva* and in social gatherings a *Vaiṣṇava*. He sees himself in all things and all things in himself. It appears, however, that the later (*uttar*) *Kaula* preferred the gross to the symbolic, just the reverse of what was fancied by the earlier (*pūrva*) *Kaula*, and *Sāmayins* alone discarded both gross sex and symbolic *yantra* and restricted themselves to mere mental imagery in using the circle for worship (*śrī cakra*). We have incontestable evidence that both the Buddhists and Nāthists, too, countenanced the *Kaula* method of self-realisation.

Orthodoxy must have been alarmed, as at the time of Mahāvīra and Buddha, by the popularity of the ascetic and homeless wandering mendicants, and so it put a virtual, though not absolute, ban on the initiation of householders by their fraternity. But it made a compromise by admitting that Tāntric initiation was essential even for brāhmaṇas, and indispensable for women and non-brāhmaṇas, who had no right to Vedic initiation. It ignored, while not extolling, the union with a Śakti (woman partner) who was not the legally married wife of the practitioner, and it preferred a married man as teacher even though he might indulge in *vāmācāra* practices in the mystic circle, where eight pairs of *yoginī* or *nāyikā* and their male partner (Bhairava) used to meet. From about the tenth century, a composite *Tantra*, drawing materials from Brāhmaṇic, Buddhist and Nāthist circles, grew up, and some deities, cults and practices became common to all of them, though the traditions did not always tally among the different communities and localities.

Let us turn now to certain other specific beliefs and speculations of the *Tantra*, and try to trace their antecedents. The *Śaiva Āgama*, the *Vaiṣṇava Saṁhitā* and *Śākta Tantra* agree on one point, namely, that a female principle representing the Śakti or energy must be associated with the Ultimate Reality or the source of locus of power considered as male. This power is not only the cause of manifestation, but is also responsible for differentiation, with the result that a diversified world in time and space, including finite individuals, comes into being because of the association of the male and the female, as in the generation of the world of living things. The general tendency of the *Tantra* is to accept the world in both its physical and mental aspects as real: only that matter of *prakṛti*, which was not accorded independent existence as in the *Sāṁkhya* system, was supposed to be under the control of the spirit and, in fact, the body was regarded as the seat of the divine in every part thereof.

The mystery of speech is an ancient tradition in India and from the Vedic times onwards speech (*vāk*) has been a prominent goddess and revealer of wisdom. Transcendental and phenomenal forms of speech (*parā, paśyanti, madhyamā* and *vaikharī*) and association of word (*śabda*) with meaning (*artha*) were speculated upon, and as ages rolled on, the power of the spoken word, whether as boons or as curses, as prayers or as incantations, grew in popular esteem. In the *Tantra* and *Āgama* a systematic attempt was made to relate sound (*nāda* or *śabda*) to reality and its different vocal symbols on seed words (*bīja-mantra*). It was believed, in fact, that just as intense imagination might cause a kind of visual hallucination and bring about the perceptual presentation of concrete figures through thinking alone, so also intense meditation on certain mystic words, which were supposed to stand for certain deities, would produce phenomena and bring before the practitioner's eye an image of the divinity concerned. They certainly brought the gods nearer to the hearts and homes of men, inspired their devotion, prompted their collective action for charity, and gave a fillip to the building of religious edifices all over the country.

# 4

# Philosophy of the Tantra and Sādhanā

TANTRA is often used in the singular, which may suggest that it is a uniform formulation of doctrine and discipline. The *Tantras* are, however, varied in their theme and expression, though they claim to have emanated from a divine source. Some call it *Āgama* while others name it as *Nigama*. The *Tantras*, being pre-eminently ways of practical realization, have necessarily to bear reference to the diverse character and competency of different aspirants and seekers. They have, accordingly, designed the framework of their theories and practices suitably adjusted to actual conditions prevailing, and evolved stages and states in the soul's journey towards its chosen ends and values.[1] The soul cannot give up its quest till it realizes all that it is potentially, in all its meaning and fulfilment, its own perfectness. This highest end has been called as *mokṣa* or liberation from bondage. Tāntric disciplines recognize and keep themselves alive to these supra-physical and supra-mental forces. The world can never be so bad (materially and spiritually) as to make those forces unavailable for the earnest seeker's reforming and transforming efforts.

Does not science illustrate the principle of polarity (*mithuna*) in ultimate as well as derivative forms? The whole creative process starts as and from polarity. We referred to Śakti elsewhere as *nāda* and *bindu*. One is the 'soil' and the other, the 'seed' for all cosmic generation. One is the extensive or expansive whole of power; the other is the intensive or concentrated whole of power. The relation of *nāda* and *bindu* is one of the hardest hurdles to negotiate in the way of understanding Tāntric principles.

The Tāntric maxim recognises that the body is the epitome of the universe and this is also the basis of medical science; it rests on the assumption that the elements forming the body cannot be dissociated from environmental elements and that by applying the laws which govern the latter, the former may be brought into order. This environmental matter is called *prakṛti* in the *Sāṁkhya* and conceived here as the Female Principle from which everything in the world is produced. *Prakṛti* is characterised by three qualities which influence and attract a number of forces conceived as *puruṣa* and it is only by the union of *prakṛti* with the *puruṣa* that creation starts in different spheres. *Prakṛti* is in a constant process of evolution and is subject to the law of cause and effect. The whole cosmos exists in a subtle form in *prakṛti* and becomes manifest in creation, and thus the unmanifest becomes manifest, the *avyakta* becomes *vyakta*.

*Tantra* could not accept idolatry because according to the very nature of its principles a deity could be adored only by one becoming the deity oneself. The idea of a separate entity for seeing God, the creator who rules the universe from heaven, is absent in *Tantra*, because according to the Tāntric view, the body of the *sādhaka* is the universe which is the abode of the desired (*iṣṭa*) and the goal to be sought (*sādhya*). The unfolding of the power of the self (*ātmaśakti*) is to be brought about by self-realisation (*ātmadarśana*) which is the aim of *sādhanā*. Śakti or power, conceived as the female principle, is in the individual and it is only for this Śakti that the existence of the individual is justified. This Śakti is conceived as existing like the power of burning in the fire throughout the created world of movable and immovable things, through the conscious and the unconscious, through the gross and the subtle. The repository of this Śakti is regarded as a static principle conceived as the Male Principle, which is symbolised by the name of God in any system. The human body is the abode of both these principles, the static Male and the dynamic Female, and the purpose of Tāntric *sādhanā* is to get these two principles in non-dual and absolute forms. For the religious aspirant in *Tantra* there is nothing apart from the body, the functioning of which is considered to belong to the same order as cosmic functioning.

The different metaphysical systems deal with the nature of Reality and the philosophic method for its apprehension; but the *Tantra* lays stress on the practical method for realizing that Reality. This practical aspect of the *sādhanā* is the essential part of the *Tantra*. Now, in this practical aspect the whole of Tāntric *sādhanā* is based on the cardinal belief that the truth is to be realized in and through the body.

The belief of the *tāntrikas* is that the ultimate truth is not an abstract principle transcending the universe but is immanent in it, and that the human body is not merely a thing in the universe — microcosm exists in relation to the macrocosm. Therefore, there is nothing in the universe which is not in the body of man. There is a perfect parallelism between the physical processes of the universe and biological processes in the body of man; with this idea, the *Tantras* try to locate sun, moon, stars, the mountains, islands and rivers of the external world within the human body. The time element of the universe in all its phases of day and night, month and year have been explained with reference to the course of the vital wind (*prāṇa* and *apāna*). The human body, with its physical structure and biological processes, represents the manifestation of the same energy which is at play in the structure and processes of the vast cosmos. The *sādhaka* should concentrate his attention on himself and realize the truth within, with the clear conviction that the truth that is realized within is the truth that pervades the universe without.

According to *yogī* (*Haṭhayogī*), the body is not only the abode of truth, but is also the best medium for realizing the truth. Different plexuses (lotuses on *cakra*), nerves and nerve-centres represent different *tattva* (essential principles), but the *tattva* represented by them lie latent until they are made potent through proper yogic culture and control.[2] Through this the physical system may be transformed into a perfect instrument for reflecting the truth.

The Hindu *Tantra* explains the Absolute Reality as having two aspects — *pravṛtti* and *nivṛtti*, which may be understood as static and dynamic or as negative and positive. In the *Tantra* these are conceived as Śiva and Śakti. Śiva is pure consciousness and is the static or the negative principle, while Śakti is the cosmic energy, world force, and as such, the dynamic or the positive aspect of Reality. But neither Śiva by himself nor Śakti by herself is the ultimate truth — they are not even separable; the highest truth is the state of neutrality produced through the union of Śiva and Śakti. When Śakti, with all her principles of illusion and defilements, dominates, the union of Śiva and Śakti, which takes place in the realm of *pravṛtti*, becomes responsible for the creation of the visible world, but when Śakti rises to Śiva in a process of introversion, their union results in a state of neutrality in infinite bliss and tranquillity. So the union that binds, may also liberate.

According to the *sādhaka* or the practical *yogī*, this *tattva* of Śiva and Śakti lies within the body of man. Śiva is residing in the highest plexus (*sahasrāra*) in the cerebral region, and Śakti is residing in the lowest plexus (*mulādhāra*); the *sādhanā* consists in raising Śakti from the lowest plexus in an upward movement till she becomes united with Śiva. Again, the right side of the body is believed to be the region of Śiva and left that of Śakti — this is the Tāntric conception of *ardhanārīśvara* (the half woman and half man). The important nerve on the right side, well-known as *piṅglā*, through which flows the *apāna vāyu* (current or air), is said to represent the principle of Śiva, while the left nerve, known as *iḍā*, through which flows the *prāṇa vāyu*, is said to represent the principle of Śakti. The *sādhanā* consists mainly in uniting Śiva-Śakti by a perfect commingling of the right and left in various ways and neutralizing their functions in a middle course called *suṣumnā*, which is the way to neutrality or perfect equilibrium of opposing currents. Man represents Śiva and woman represents Śakti; the perfect bliss that results from a strict discipline and yogic control of their union leads one to perfect tranquillity, which is the state of the Absolute.

In the human body, the central great axis (Mount Meru) is surrounded by seven islands (the vital force, blood, flesh, fat, bones, marrow and so on), as well as seers, sages, gods, goddesses, intelligence, all the stars and planets, sacred places, shrines and presiding deities, the sun and the moon, the agents of creation and destruction. These also move through the body, as do the five great elements of space, air, fire, water and earth. All the beings that exist in all worlds are to be found within the body, surrounding the central great axis.

In this body, which is called *brahmāṇḍa* (the egg or the aura of *Brahman*), the microcosm, there is the nectar-rayed moon, in its proper place, on the top of the spinal column. With its face downward, it rains nectar day and night. The ambrosia from the moon has two subtle parts: one of these nourishes the body like the water of the heavenly river Gaṅgā, descending as a subtle channel on the left side while the other ray of ambrosia, brilliant as the milk, enters the central nerve of the spinal column in order to maintain and recreate the moon in its proper place on top of the central great axis.

At the lower region of the great axis of Meru is the Sun, located within the body itself. From the inner sun situated at the naval, a subtle channel emanates to the right side of the body and carries the solar fluid upward by the power of its rays. This nerve on the right side is another form of the sun and moves through the body, swallowing up vital secretions and ultimately, leading the spirit to liberation. The lord of creation and destruction is the sun, which moves through the vessel of the body.

In the human body there are several thousand subtle channels, but the principle ones are fourteen in number. Of these, three are particularly important: *iḍā* (to the left), *piṅgalā* (to the right) and *suṣumnā* (in the centre). Of these three, *suṣumnā* alone is the highest and most beloved of the *yogī*; all other subtle channels are subordinate to it. The nerve[3] called *iḍā* is on the left side, coiling around the *suṣuṁnā* and going to the right nostril. The nerve *piṅgalā* is on the right side, coiling around the central channel and entering the left nostril. He who knows this microcosm of the body and experiences its mysteries reaches the highest state.

Esoteric teachings declare that if one truly wishes to advance spiritually, one must work consciously to activate the subtle body. Though the basic ingredients and raw energies exist in everyone, they must be focused and channelled consciously. The emotions and the mind should be brought to bear on the conscious evocation of an all-powerful subtle body, which can then serve as a source of strength, intelligence and transcendence. This is one of the most important secrets of the Tāntric tradition.

The highest of all values is love, and its fountain is in our body. The worship must start with the body of man. In the mortal frame resides the immortal.

Physical love is an instrument of training for realising the higher spiritual love. When that stage is reached all differences disappear. The seeker reaches a state of beatitude and dissolves into an endless sea of beauty, joy and love.[4] The body pines for love. It is the carnal passion, sensuous desire which seeks appeasement in the coils of flesh. Sexual union is an sacred *yoga* which, though involving enjoyment of all the sensual pleasures, gives the ultimate realise. It is a path to liberation.[5] This is nothing to be ashamed of. It is a manifestation on the plane of life of the cosmic attraction which gives mobility to all non-living phenomena from the electrons to the galaxies. The cosmic attraction is expressed in animal flesh as desire for physical unity. Nature is beaming with love, so is man. Our sophisticated and repressive culture has sought to make stable this dynamic vital surge. The lake of love is below the waist. There lies dormant the seed of spiritual growth. The culture of erotics or physical love under right directions raises it to a higher plane, where the subject finds complete identity with the object, where beauty, joy and love surpass all empirical limits, where worldly fear and pain lose their sting. The union of man and woman is a symbol of eternal communion and an awareness of oneness through duality. From the Tāntric point of view the consummation is the human being, man and woman making up one unit. It is not limited to the physical plane. It is the state of perfect beatitude when the mind has reached the highest aesthetic level and sees the world as a vast ocean of love. The union of male and female principles is like the mating of Heaven and Earth, Dyau and Prithivi where the two become one (*Dyāvāprithivi*). Human beings could not comprehend this secret and have, therefore, become mortals. By knowing it the path to Immortality is opened. The philosophy of life is the reconciliation of different contradictions which paves the way to the Absolute.

The cardinal desire of man and woman for each other, for example, and the fact of their physical union become 'carnal' on the relative and pragmatic plane, where the body is 'material' and the soul 'spiritual', and there is a perennial conflict between the flesh and the spirit. The distinction is a valid one and may be of value on the conventional plane. Man must be able to realize that nothing exists and functions except Śiva and Śakti. All action is play (*līlā*) of Śiva and Śakti. After this realization nothing remains 'carnal' or 'gross'. Everything becomes an expression of the Perfect Being (consciousness-bliss).

## References

1. S.B. Dasgupta, *Obscure Religious Cults*, Calcutta, 1959, p. 34; John Wood Raffe, *Principles of Tantras*, Pt. I, Madras, 1952, Preface; Baldev Upadhyaya, *Bhārtīya Darśana* (in Hindi), Varanasi, 1966, pp. 429-30; Lalmani Joshi, *Studies in Buddhist Culture of India*, Banaras, 1967, pp. 305-7; Nagendra Nath Upadhyaya, *Bauddha Kāpālik Sādhanā Aur Sāhitya*, (in Hindi), Allahabad, 1983, pp. 43-5.

2. The centre of power in the human body is not an innovation of the Tāntric. It has its root in the cosmic law of evolution and is revealed to mankind for their salvation; the centre of power is the cause from which the five sheaths arise. These are — sheath of food (*annamaya kośa*), sheath of life (*prāṇamaya kośa*), sheath of lower mind (*manomaya kośa*), sheath of higher mind (*vijñānamaya kośa*) and sheath of bliss (*ānandmaya kośa*). *Ānandmaya kośa* arises from the elements, earth, water and fire. Earth and water produce food, which is assimilated by fire and converted into the substance which forms the body it nourishes. Earth, water and fire are the presiding elements in *mūlādhāra*, *svādhiṣṭhāna* and *maṇipūra* centres respectively. They became the objects of concentration in the first place, as by awakening the *kula-kuṇḍalini*, the *sādhaka* first meets *mūlādhāra*, then *svādhiṣṭhāna* and then *maṇipūra*. The *prāṇamaya kośa* arises from *anāhata* and *viśuddha* in centre, in which vital air and space (ether) respectively preside, includes the ten senses which form the vital breath. It is a subtle form of manifestation. The *manomaya kośa* is evolved from the *ājñā cakra*, which is the centre the mind. The mind is the faculty which discriminates between the physical sensations of the five perceptive senses. The *vijñānamaya kośa* arises from the *bindu* and *nāda*. It directly reflects the intelligence (*buddhi*) of the material body (*kāraṇa śarīra*) or the principles of five senses of man and undifferentiated nature (*prakṛti*). In *sahasrāra* is *ānandamaya kośa*.

The different kinds of energy that we find working in nature are different expressions of one great energy. This is, in scientific terminology, known as correlation of forces.

3. In the common parlance, the word *nāḍī* has some ambiguities. In the Indian indigenous system of medicine (*āyurveda*) the word *nāḍī* means pulse, but the meaning taken in the yogic tradition comes very near the word 'nerve'. It is right to use the word *nāḍī* as nerve.

4. The Buddha immediately after his experience of Enlightenment is known to have uttered a strophe expressing a similar comparison. "All pleasures of worldly Joys, All which are known among the gods, compared with the joy of Nirvāṇa, Are not as its sixteenth part". (W.W. Reckhill, *The Life of Buddha*, reprint, Varanasi, 1972, p. 33; *Bṛhadāraṇyaka Upaniṣad*, IV.3.32 and IV.2.32; *Taittirīya Upaniṣad*, II.8; Paul Deussen, *The Philosophy of the Upaniṣad*, reprint, New Delhi, 1979, p. 143).

5. S.B. Dasgupta, *An Introduction to Tantrik Buddhism*, Calcutta, 1950, pp. 144-5.

# 5

# Evolution of the Tantras

THE *Tantra* denotes a cultural discipline in a wider sense, and when used in a limited sense, it is spiritual knowledge of a technical nature. The Tāntric literature essentially represents a very important part of Indian spiritual experience, so far as its practical aspect is concerned. Whatever might have been the nature of sacrifice in the early Vedic period, it developed into highly mystical rituals in course of time and the essence of Vedic religion remained throughout ritualistic. The religious attitude in the *Tantras* is, fundamentally, the same as in the Vedic ritual.

The Tāntric *sādhanā* also concerns ascendancy over the force of nature by exoteric rituals of Vedic type as well as by esoteric rituals involving the yogic practice, its aim being the union of the two principles, *jīva* and *ātamā*, Śiva and Śakti, *prakṛti* and *puruṣa*, *prajñā* and *upāya*, *śūnyatā* and *karuṇā*, *nāda* and *bindu*, etc. The *Tantra* used new symbols and tended to simplify the Vedic rituals to some extent. A similar esotericism is to be found in other religious systems. With this point of view in mind, it may be concluded that the *Tantras* emerged out of the Vedic religion and developed subsequently as a distinct type of esoteric knowledge, with greater emphasis on esoteric sacrifice.

*Tantra*, according to some, is the culmination of the esoteric science of *Vedānta* and *Sāṁkhya*. It asserts the ultimate reality of Śiva (b*rahman*) and the validity of the world as an expression of his Śakti. The origin and development of the *Tantra* as a special class of literature and as a special mode of *sādhanā* was intimately connected with the rise of Śaivism, with the *Sāṁkhya* supplying them a philosophical background.

There are three classes of *Tantras* — *dakṣiṇa, vāma* and *madhyama.* All the three promulgate profound matters concerning *tattva* and *mantra. Tattva* means the science of the cosmic principles, while *mantra* means the science of the mystic sound (mysticism by its very nature transcending sectarianism and regionalism in the highest stages of its development).

*Vāmācāra* is based on the profound knowledge of the 'return current' (*nivṛtti*), which seeks to reverse the process of creating and maintaining the bonds of propensities and conventions in which the *jīva* or soul has been held as a *paśu.* It must be clearly perceived that in this path, the aspirant has to make use of a certain kind of ritual (*pañcatattva*) which, leading admittedly to some abuse in unsuitable cases and conditions, has made the whole cult of *tantra* suspect in the judgement of those who do not understand and discriminate. Even those who understood nothing of the 'return current' (reversing process) got themselves involved in the theory and practice of the left path. Curiously enough, a full-blooded counterpart of the essentials of the *tāntrika pañcatattva* worship can be traced to the Vedic worship.[1]

The end of the *sādhaka* is, to attain pure and perfect *cit* or consciousness. This is also a stage of perfect being and perfect bliss. In the *Tantra,* as also in the *Vedānta,* the word for this perfect state is *saccidānanda.*

Every kind of duality must be reduced to zero. Man and woman, for example, may be sublimated into cosmic principles, polar to each other in the outgoing aspect of the cosmic process, but identified and unified Śiva-Śakti in reality which is experienced in the reversing of the outgoing current. In reversing the process, we have to bring the two complements (poles) 'together' so as to reaffirm and realize the identical whole. The so-called 'erotic' symbolism is sublimated as the creative union of Śiva and Śakti, the thrill of the act of union being *nāda*; and the 'seed' that issues from the union is *bindu*. In the *vāmācāra* path, which under certain very stringent conditions prescribes to the *sādhnā* or ritual readjustment with woman, such sublimation of the so-called 'carnal' act has to be effected till the supreme *advaita* Śiva-Śakti experience with its perfect *ānanda* or bliss is attained.[2]

The Śiva-Śakti school of *Tantra* is a presentation of *Advaita Vedānta* from the point of view of a science of practical application and realization. It is a *śāstra* of *sādhanā* and *siddhi*. Pure and undifferentiated consciousness is, of course, affirmed as the basic aspect of Reality. Perfect experience is experience of the whole, that is, of consciousness as Being and consciousness as the power to become.

According to the *Tantra* Śiva has two aspects: *nirguṇa* (attributeless) and *saguṇa* (with attributes). As *nirguṇa*, Śiva is transcendent and therefore dissociated from *prakṛti* or Śakti; and as a *saguṇa*, Śiva is associated with Śakti. It is in the latter aspect of Śiva that Śakti emanates; from that, *nāda* (sound) and out of the *nāda*, *bindu*. This conception can be put in another way. At the time of final dissolution (*pralaya*) everything is withdrawn into the supreme Śakti. Therefore, when Śakti, which is substance (*tattva*), approaches the light, which is knowledge (*cit*), there arises in the former the desire to create (*vicikarṣa*). It bursts and divides itself, and out of that division arise the *bindu*, *nāda* and *bīja*. *Bindu* partakes of the nature of Śiva (*jñāna*), *bīja* is Śakti, and *nāda* is the relation between Śiva and Śakti as the stimulator and stimulated (*kṣobhya*). When the *bindu* bursts, an inchoate volume of sound is produced. This sound is called *śabda brahman*, which is the *caitanya* (stress towards manifestation in all beings) pervading all creation, and is the source of letters of the alphabet, of words, and of other sounds by which thoughts are exchanged. Sounds have meanings and both are inseparable.

The *jiva* as a centre represents a certain phase and position in the evolution-involution process of perfect *cit-śakti* by which a universe arises and is withdrawn. Evolution means the patent, kinetic aspect, while involution means the latent, static or potential. Every form of being is thus a kinetic-static composite. The polarity of static/kinetic is everywhere. The gross, subtle and causal forces, is the body of the *jīva*; the static pole of creating, sustaining and resolving Śakti is represented by the *kuṇḍalinī* (coiled serpent-power). It will be seen that the gross comes out of the subtle in the process of unfolding, and when it is reversed the gross disappears in the subtle. In this way the *sādhaka* begins with a gross material accessory (image) and rises step-by-step to that which is beyond word and speech.

The *Tantras* lay down different types of practices for the attainment of the highest aim of human existence by one living the ordinary life of a householder. The *Tantra* falls under five broad categories — *Śaiva, Śākta, Vaiṣṇava, Sūrya* and *Gāṇapatya.* These are called *pañcopāsanā* and each of these has its own way of worship. Scholars have differences of opinion as to how many *Tantras* there actually are. According to some, there are as many as sixty-four branches of *Tantras*.

The *Tantra* classifies the *sādhaka* under three categories. The *sādhaka* with divine (*divya*) disposition (*bhāva*) forms an important factor in the process of *sādhanā*. The *sādhaka* with animal (disposition) is a slave of lust, anger, greed, pride, illusion and envy. He can hardly be expected to see, beyond the gross (*sthūla*) or material aspect of the things, the *vīra*, who is fighting the six enemies (passions) who obstruct the way of spiritual advancement. The *sādhaka* of *divya* disposition is, as a result of his practices in his previous birth, endowed with qualities which make him almost divine.

Closely connected with these dispositions are the seven rules (*ācāra*) of conduct, which are given in *Kulārṇava Tantra* as follows: *Veda, Vaiṣṇava, Śaiva, Daksiṇa, Vāma, Siddhānta* and *Kaula*. The aspirant rises step-by-step through these different rules till he reaches the highest. The first four stages (ways) are — cleanliness of the body and mind, devotion (*bhakti*), knowledge (*jñāna*), *daksiṇa*, the fourth stage in which the gains acquired in the preceding three stages are consolidated. This is followed by *vāma* which is the stage of renunciation. This does not mean the practice of rites with woman (*vāmā*) as has been said by the detractors of *Tantra*. *Vāma* is the reverse of *daksiṇa*; it means the path of renunciation. If a woman is at all associated in this practice, she is there to help in the path of renunciation, and not for animal gratification. A woman as such is an object of great veneration to all schools of Tāntric *sādhaka* (seekers). She is considered to be the embodiment on earth of the supreme Śakti who pervades the universc. The sixth stage, *siddhānta* denotes that in which the aspirant comes to a difinitive conclusion after deliberate consideration as to the relative merits of the path of enjoyment and that of renunciation. By pursuing the path of renunciation, he reaches the final stage of *kaula*. This is the stage in which *kaula* or *brahman* becomes reality to him. The first three of these seven stages — *Veda, Vaiṣṇava* and *Śaiva* — belong to *paśubhāva, daksiṇa* and *vāma* belong to *vīrabhāva* and the last two belong to *divyabhāva*.

The disciple should always bear in mind that his teacher is immortal. The true teacher is the Brahmā or Śiva or primordial Śakti. This does not mean that the human teacher is so; he is the channel through which the spirit of supreme *Brahman* descends. The position of the human teacher is one of very great responsibility, which does not end with initiation. *Guru* (teacher) is called the physician of the soul. He is the form and the embodiment of supreme power.[3] The place of *guru* and his *dīkṣā* are thus of vital importance. *Gurutattva* may, and often does, operate through a human body.

It has already been said that there are five aspects in all *Tāntrika* teaching. Leaving apart the first four, the fifth aspect is beyond all description and all worship; for that is the state where the worshipper and the worshipped become one.

The aspirant who partakes of the five *tattva* to please the deity within him incurs no demerit. Such a man looks upon wine and meat as Śakti and Śiva, and is fully alive to the fact that the wine of which he is about to partake will make manifest the bliss that is *brahman* within him. Wine is drunk with appropriate rites and with the recitation of an appropriate *mantra*, it is suffused with the nectar of the moon shining in the forehead of Śiva. It is the ocean bliss and makes the aspirant think of his oneness with Śiva. *Mantras* have a threefold meaning: the gross one is the actual drinking of wine; the subtle one is the drinking of the nectar which flows from the union of *kuṇḍalinī* with Śiva in the *sahasrāra*; and the third (the transcendent) one is the nectar of happiness arising from the realization of the union of the *parā* Śiva and the *parā* Śakti. The *Kulārṇava Tantra* says that the wine which is gladness, is the nectar that flows from the union of the *kuṇḍalinī* Śakti with Śiva at the *sahasrāra* in the head. And those who do not drink this nectar are mere winebibbers. The man who kills by the sword of *jñāna*, the animal of merit and demerit, leads his mind to the supreme. Śiva is said to be a true eater of flesh. That man truly takes fish who controls all his senses and places them in his *ātmā*; others are mere killers of animals. The man who enjoys this Śakti is said to be a true enjoyer of Śakti. He experiences the bliss which arises out of the union of supreme Śakti and *ātmā*, which is the true union; others are no better than fornicators. The term for the fifth *tattva* is derived from the word *maithuna*. Since nothing in the world of experience happens without the combination of two things, even consciousness is impossible without it. *Maithuna*[4] symbolizes the unity which is behind all this duality, which is beyond ordinary human comprehension and which the liberated in life (*jīvan-mukta*) alone can apprehend. The attainment of this *tattva* requires the offering of the sense of duality before the chosen deity and this is done so that the underlying oneness may be realized. This is the true significance of the fifth *tattva*.

Ultimate Reality is visualized as supreme non-duality. In its phenomenalization, or in the process of becoming, it manifests two aspects conceived of as negative and the positive, the static and the dynamic. The two polar aspects of reality are represented in the Hindu *Tantra* as Śiva and Śakti and in Buddhist *Tantra* as *upāya* (method) and *prajñā* (knowledge) *vajra* and *kamala*. All schools of Tāntrism hold that these two polar metaphysical principles are manifested in the material world in the form of the male and female, and the ultimate goal of all esoteric disciplines is to destroy all principles of dualism and to attain the final state of non-duality or return to a primordial state of non-differentiation. In different esoteric systems, this state of non-duality is variously called the stage of *advaya, maithuna, yuganaddha, kaula, yāmala, yugala, samarasa, paramasukha, nirvāṇa, sahaja* or *sahajānanda* or simply the state of *samādhi*. It is conceived of as *ānanda* (bliss) or *mahāsukha* (great bliss) and enlightenment (*bodhicitta*). The *sādhanā* to reach the Ultimate Reality consists of the union of the male and the female which gives highest pleasure and supreme joy or bliss. But the sexual union ordinarily perfomed gives only temporary pleasure. So, in the Tāntric *sādhanā* it is converted into a ritual. The male and the female copulate as god and goddess — Śiva and Śakti, *upāya* and *prajñā* or any divine pair depending upon the affiliation of the *sādhaka*. One should worship god after becoming one himself. The *sādhaka*, thinking of himself as god and his female partner as representing the goddess, performs the sexual act.

## References

1. Describing the supreme state of virtue, the *Ṛgveda* (IX.113.11)

speaks of the following motifs of the most exalted felicity: immortality in that realm where there are joys and delights, enjoyment combined with felicity and extreme fulfilment of the desire of *kāma*. The husband wraps his body in the garment of the wife (*Rgveda*, X.85:30), "Come, come you, O darling come! Let you consume this food and unite with me". (*Atharvaveda*, XX.135.11 & 13).

Those who shiver at the thought of Tāntric *maithuna* rites will perhaps be surprised to learn that in the Vedic texts sexual union is identified with the *yajña* or sacrifice. Numerous passage from the *Brāhmaṇas* (*Śatapatha Brāhmaṇa*, V.1.3.23; III, 2.1.2; IV.6.7.9-10; VI.5.3.5; XI.6.2.10 & J. Eggeling, trans. in *SBI*, Vol. XLIV, p. 316 onwards; *Kauśitakī Brāhmaṇa*, XVI.5 and *Jaiminīya Brāhmaṇa*, II.285) equate sexual union with *yajña*. The blissful condition has been epitomised by the word bliss (*ānanda*) and in the *Upaniṣad* the essence of all human knowledge is comprehended under this concept, identified with the Ultimate Reality. Thus it is put in the *Bṛhadāraṇyaka Upaniṣad* — "As a man fully embraced by his beloved wife knows nothing that is within, nothing that is without, so this *puruṣa*, when fully embraced by the supreme self, knows nothing that is within, nothing that is without. Verily, that is its form in which all the desires are satisfied, in which all desires become the self, and which is free from desires and devoid of grief " (IV.3.21); again, this *Upaniṣad* says: Woman is the sacrificial fire, the lips of her *yoni* the fuel, the hairs around them the smoke and vagina itself the flame. The act of penetration is lighting, the feeling of the pleasure is the sparks. In this fire the gods offer up semen-seed, and from this offering man is born. It states again — the lower portion of a women (*upastha*) is to be conceived as the sacrificial altar (*vedī*), the pubic hair (*lomāni*) as the sacrificial grass, the outer skin (*bahiścarman*) as the floor for pressing of the Soma plants (*adhisavāna*), and the two labia of the vulva (*muskan*) as the innermost fire. Verily, indeed, as great as the world of him who sacrifices with the strength-libation sacrifice, is the world of him who practises sexual union, knowing this (*Bṛhadāraṇyaka*, VI.4.2-3). In the *Chāndogya Upaniṣad* we have the following passage — the *maithuna* of male and female is this syllable *oṁ*. Verily, when a *maithuna* comes together the two sexes fulfil the desire (*kāma*) of each other (1.1.6) equivalent to this mystic concept of *oṁ*. Again this *Upaniṣad* states that — one summons; that is *hiṁkāra*. He makes request, that is a *prastāva*. Together with women he lies down; that is an *udgīthā*. He lies upon the woman; that is *pratihāra*. He comes to an end; that is *nidhāna*. He comes to a finish, that is *nidhāna*. This is the *vāmadeya sāmanas* woven upon copulation. (*Chāndogya Upaniṣad*, II.1.3) Indeed the highest value to the fleshly union is accorded by the Vedic thinkers who view procreation as a sacrifice. Indeed, the sexual basis of mortal creation is itself glorified as a perfect *yajña* which links us every moment with the divine immortality. A Tāntric origin in the imagery can hardly be overlooked. The remaining four *tattava* may also be found in Vedic texts — *Ṛgveda*, I.22.20 to 21 (*mudrā*), IV.40.5 (*madirā*), X.184.1-2 (*maithuna*), I.154.2 (*māṁsa*), VII.59.12 (*mastya*); *Taittirīya Āraṇyaka*, X.1.15.

2. Hara Prasad Shastri, *Advaya Sangraha*, Gayakwada Oriental Series, Baroda, 1927, p. 28.

3. Gopi Nath Kaviraj, *Tāntric Vāṅgamaya Aur Sākta-Dṛṣṭi*, (in Hindi), Patna, 1963; Nagendra Nath Upadhyay, *Bauddha Kāpālika Sādhanā Aur Sāhitya* (in Hindi), Allahabad, 1983, pp. 168-90; Bhagawati Prasad Singh, *Manīṣī Kī Lokayātrā* (in Hindi), Varanasi, 1980.

4. P.C. Bagachi, *Studies in the Tantras*, Part I, Calcutta, 1939, pp. 87-92.

# 6

# Concept of Śakti and Śāktism

ŚĀKTISM is a direct offshoot of the primitive Mother Goddess cult which was a prominent feature of the religion of the ancient agricultural people who are referred to as the Indus Valley people. It is clear that the *Śākta* religion developed in a female-dominated society where rituals based upon the fertility image played a very significant role. The concept of the Mother Goddess would have developed in course of time. The concept became varied in nature depending upon the degree of culture attained by separate communities at different times. An evidence to this is the various types of the goddess cults still prevailing in different regions and among diverse people.

On the basis of the Vedic texts, it can be said that the contemporary civilization was mainly based on pastoral economy, patriarchal social organisation, natural gods and sacrificial cults. The Vedic texts reveal the existence of a number of material cultures of different grades under a common tradition and ideology. These traits are historical realities which can be traced, identified and documented, and which as an undifferentiated cultural complex originally stood in opposition to the Tāntric outlook — wherein the female figure dominated — inherited from the pre-Vedic way of life.[1] Many rituals designed to secure the fertility of[2] fields, mainly sexual in character, found their way into the Vedic texts and became the visible portions of the Tāntric iceberg. The evidence relating to sexual rituals and their connection with agriculture and the cult of the Mother Goddess cannot be completely brushed aside and it is interesting to note that in almost every period, the Vedic literature shows traces of sexual rituals and a pattern of sexual behaviour that differed from accepted norms. Reference has also been made to the use of five *ma-kāras* (*pañca ma-kāra*) in Vedic rites.[3] It is a fact that the Vedic texts contain many Tāntric ideas and practices. Even the Vedic sacrificial cult was not basically different from those of the *Tantras*. In the *Brāhmaṇa* literature sexual union was not only regarded as the means of achieving spiritual happiness, but it was also identified with the sacrifice itself.[4]

In the *Upaniṣads*, we come across views regarding the origin of life and the universe.[5] The doctrines of *bhūta*, *yoni* and *puruṣa* are mentioned, with the term *prakṛti* being used later as a substitute for *bhūta* and *yoni*. These four concepts denote the earlier stages of the evolution of the Tāntric ideas. The creation of the world was viewed in terms of human procreation and that is why supreme emphasis was laid upon the concept of *prakṛti* or the female principle of creation. However, with the recognition of the role of the male in the process of procreation, we come across the development of the concept of *puruṣa* or Male Principle where this male element is still inactive and passive. The doctrine of *bhūta* suggests that everything in the world is created by the combination of five material elements, *viz.*, earth, water, fire, air and space which are also known as the five *mahābhūta*. The first four have colour and touchability whereas the fifth, space is the container of sound. These figure in all forms of ancient Indian thought including the *Tantras*.

In popular belief Tāntrism is same as Śāktism; this belief is not without some historical foundation. It is in the *Śākta* religion that the Tāntric ideas and practices have found the most favourable ground for their meaningful survival and development. The most notable feature of the *Śākta* Tāntric idea is that the supreme being is female which is worshipped under different names and forms. In other religious systems also there is evidently a place for the goddess but the difference is that she is conceived of as the wife or consort of the male god; where the Tāntric influence is greater she is conceived of as his inherent Śakti, inseparable from his own entity or self. In Śāktism she is supreme, other gods having a subordinate position. *Śākta* religion emphasises the motherhood of god. It is not equally absurd and illogical to assign a particularly definite sex to god. Eternal and Infinite *brahman* is formless and sexless; again, all forms are His forms, and all sexes are His and have evolved from him. So, he is the both the Mother and the Father of the Universe. The whole creation is an act of emergence from *brahman* (we may say *brahman* Father and Mother); what we love most, like most, and revere most, we can think and call that *brahman*. Śāktism has preferred to represent Eternal *brahman* as Eternal Mother of the Universe (there is nothing more deep and more disinterested than a mother's love).[6]

Śakti is the root of all existence. It is from Śakti that the universe has evolved; it is by Śakti that it is sustained; and it is into Śakti that it is finally resolved. Śakti is the same as the supreme being (*parabrahman*). The supreme being is existence (*sat*), consciousness (*cit*) and bliss (*ānanda*) and Śakti denotes these three aspects. Śakti is essentially absolute *sat* + *cit* + *ānanda*. Śakti is neither male nor female, but partakes of the characteristics of both. Without Śakti nothing can live and move; 'being' is not possible without Śakti.

The manifest Śakti is the power which is the object of adoration, prayer and praise. Śakti is life, intelligence and consciousness. No existence can be superior to Her. The aspects of Śakti are inseparable, and one is not inferior to the other. It is *Śakti* (power) which creates, Śakti which sustains, Śakti which withdraws into Her fathomless womb as if into the place of innumerable worlds in infinite space. Indeed she is space itself and contains every being therein. She is *māyā*[7] (illusion), because *māyā* is a part of Her nature. She is *avidyā* (ignorance) because she binds and she is *vidyā* (knowledge) because she holds the light which illumines the path of return; she is *mahā-māyā* (great-illusion) because she dominates *māyā*; and she is *mahā vidyā* (supreme knowledge). She is the mother in whose sweet and soothing bosom the way-worn piligrim finds his eternal rest.

The Divine Mother is thus the cause of bondage as well as of liberation. She is in all things and all things are in Her. Both centrifugal and centripetal forces are in Her. The human ego has the privilege to choose either of these spiritual forces to work out its destiny. The three aspects of Śakti which constitute the Trinity of the Hindu religion are *ichhā-śakti* (volition), *kriyā-śakti* (administration) and *jñāna-śakti* (cognition). These are the three powers which direct the evolution, sustenance and the involution of the universe. Being Śakti (*kalā*), she is associated with an eternal bond. *Kalā* means absolute transcendental power. The first transformation of this Śakti is *ichhā* (will). Śakti emerges from the supreme being at the beginning of creation. This appearance of Śakti is like the revival of the memory of one who rises from deep sleep. The supreme being and Śakti are both of the nature of *cit* or pure consciousness, but since Śakti acts on everything, it sometimes appears as knowledge and sometimes as an action, according to the nature of things themselves. According to the Śakti Tāntric viewpoint, Śakti is inherent in Śiva as the power of burning is inherent in the fire. The supposed five faces of Śiva[8] — Īśāna, Tatapuruṣa, Sadyojāta, Vāmadeva and Aghora — symbolise the functioning of Śakti in spheres of consciousness (*cit*), bliss (*ānanda*), will (*ichhā*), knowledge (*jñāna*) and action (*kriyā*) respectively. With the opening of Śakti the universe appears; with her closing it disappears.

Almost all forms of Indian religious systems were greately influenced by Tāntric ideas and practices.[9] But it was only in Śāktism that the Tāntric ideas and practices were able to flourish. The human body is the microcosm of the universe; therefore, sexual process is responsible for the creation of the world. Though theoretically Śiva and Śakti are inseparable like fire and its burning power, in the case of creation they have dual roles. Śiva is the male principle of creation and Śakti the female, and their union is the process of creation; the former is passive and the latter active. This reminds us of the *prakṛti* and *puruṣa* doctrine[10] of *Sāṁkhya* wherein *vimarśa-prakāśa* has no practical value just as without *prakṛti*, *puruṣa* is quite inactive. That is why it is stated that without Śakti, Śiva is no better than a corpse (*śava*).[11] The nature of creation is like a wheel continually revolving. Śakti, having issued from its source, completes a cycle of creation, preservation, destruction and then returns to its source again. This process is in motion throughout the ages. The Tāntrics imitate this process through the symbolical union with their female partners.[12] Śakti's return to Her source is imitated by the rite of *ṣaṭcakrabheda*. Śakti resides at the same time in the microcosm as well as the macrocosm; she remains latent as the serpent-power in the *mūlādhāracakra* of human body. This is to be awakened and sent to the *sahasrāra* (the highest cerebral region) through different nerve cycles situated within the body. This is how Śakti meets Her source.

Only a few followers are entitled to the rites of *ṣaṭcakrabheda* and *pañca ma-kāra*[13] (five Ms.). *Vāmācāra*, *siddhāntācāra* and *kaulācāra* are more or less the same but among them *kaulācāra* worship is considered to be the best. Herein, the *kaulastrī* is worshipped in different ways (*kaulastrī* does not mean a housewife). A woman is specially chosen as the Female Principle for worship, and in the worship the five *ma-kāras* are essential. All women are symbolised as Śakti. Wine and meat are the symbols of Śakti and Śiva respectively and their consumer is Bhairava, it is stated in *Kulārṇava Tantra*. When these three are united, salvation is attained in the form of bliss. The drinking of wine is the symbol of drinking the essence derived from the Śiva and

Śakti *sāmarasya* (equilibrium) in the *sahasrāra* (highest cerebral region).[14] Sexual union is the symbol of the union of Śiva and Śakti. This takes place when the goddess after having pierced all the *kulapatha* (way of Kaula) in the *mūlādhāra* (earth), *svādhiṣṭhāna* (water), *maṇipūra* (fire), *anāhata* (air), *viśuddha* (space) and *ājñā* (mind), enjoys the company of her consort in the *sahasrāra.*[15] *Cakra* is the symbol of the universe.[16] There is an explanation, based primarily on the philosophical concepts of *Upaniṣad,* according to which the function of *cakra* can be defined as the principle of life and energy.

*Mūlādhāra-cakra* is the first nerve-plexus, which is so-called for being the root of *suṣumnā* nerve where *kuṇḍalinī-śakti* rests. It is in the region midways between the genitals and the anus. Whatever its position inside the body may be, it is symbolically viewed as a lotus with four petals representing four forms of bliss (*parama, sahaja, yoga* and *vīra*) and four letters (*va, sa, śa, ṣa*). Each letter conveys a particular sound (*śabda*) or Śakti, and as such they are manifestations of the *kuṇḍalinī.* In the pericarp is the square *dharā maṇḍala* (the supposed earth) and within it the *dharā-bīja* (the seed of earth symbolised by letter *la*). In the pericarp, there is also the lightning like triangle (*yoni,* female organ) inside which are the vital wind of passion (*kāma-vāyu*) and vital fluid (*kāma-bīja*) symbolised by letter *klīṁ.* Above this is the *Svayaṁbhū liṅga* round which *kuṇḍalinī*[17] is coiled. This *cakra* is associated with the *pṛthvī tattva* (Earth).

*Svādhiṣṭhāna-cakra* is the second lotus of six petals which is situated on the spinal centre of the region at the root of the genitals. Six petals are letters *ba, bha, ma, ya, ra* and *la.* Just as the *mūlādhāra* is associated with earth which is indicated by the octagonal pericarp with the half moon in the centre, *Svādhiṣṭhāna* denotes the region of water.[18]

*Maṇipūra-cakra* is at the centre of the naval region. On it is placed a lotus of ten petals. In the pericarp of the lotus is the red region of fire, which is triangular in shape. Outside it, on its three sides, are the three *svastika* signs. Within the triangle is the *bīja* of fire symbolised in the letter *ra.*[19]

*Anāhata-cakra* is in the region of the heart. It is a lotus of twelve petals on which are letters from *ka* to *tha*, with the *bindu* above them. Its pericarp is the hexagonal and it represents *vāyu-maṇḍala*; it is connected with the element of air.[20]

*Viśuddha-cakra* is at the base of the throat with sixteen petals of a smoky purple hue. Its filaments are ruddy, and the sixteen vowels having *bindu* above are seen on the petals. It is connected with the elements of space (ether). Inside it is the *candra-maṇḍala* and above it is the *bīja ha*. This *bīja* is Sadāśiva in his *ardhanārīśvara* aspect.[21]

*Ājñā-cakra* is situated in the forehead between the eyebrows (between the two eyes). It is in the region of the mind. It is white and has two petals on which are the letters *ha* and *kṣa*. It contains, within a triangle, the inner soul (*antarātmā*) lustrous like flame on its four sides, floating in air; these sparks surrounding a light make everything visible between *mūla* and *brahmarandhra*. Above this, again, is *manas*, above which is *haṁsa* within whom *parama* Śiva stays with Śakti.[22]

The highest cerebral region, at the top of *suṣumnā nāḍī*, is known as *sahasrāra*. It is conceived as a lotus of thousand petals. It is white with red filaments. The fifty letters of the alphabet from *a* to *la* are repeated twenty times around the thousand petals. On its pericarp is a *haṁsa* and above it is *parama* Śiva himself. Above these are the *sūrya* (Sun) and *candra-maṇḍalas*. In the latter (*candra-maṇḍala*) there is a lightning like triangle within which is the sixteenth *kalā* of Moon. Its subtle aspect is known as *nirvāṇa-kalā* within which is *parā-bindu* symbolising Śiva and Śakti. The Śakti of this *parā-bindu* is known as *nirvāṇa-śakti*, which is light and exists in the form of *haṁsa.*[23]

It may be pointed out that the *padma* or *cakra*[24] were originally conceived of in terms of human anatomy for the purpose of physiological study. The *cakra* commencing with the *mūlādhāra* and going upwards, was associated with the sacral (sacrum = Δ), prostatic, epigastric, cardiac, laryngeal and cavernous plexuses and the *sahasrāra* with the medulla. At a subsequent stage, in conformity with the Tāntric idea that the human body is the microcosm of the universe, worldly objects (i.e., sun, moon, mountain, rivers) were connected with these *cakras*. Each *cakra* was again thought to represent the gross and subtle elements. The gross element of earth and subtle elements like cohesion and stimulation of the sense of smell, arise from the region, *mūlādhāra*. In *svādhiṣṭhāna*, the gross element is water and the subtle elements include contraction and stimulation of the sense of taste; *maṇipūra* involves the gross element of fire and the related subtle elements are expansion, production of heat and stimulation of sight, sense of colour and form; in *anāhata*, the gross element is air and the subtle elements connected with it are general movement and stimulation of sense of touch. In *viśuddha*, the related gross element is space and the related subtle element is the stimulation of sense of hearing; *ājñā* identifies the gross element of mind, with the subtle elements being the mental faculties. These subtle elements, as *tattvas*, are connected with the different organs, main and subsidiary — smell with nose and taste (*rasa*) with tongue and hand, form (*rūpa*) and colour with eyes and anus, touch (*sparśa*) with skin and penis, and *śabda* or sound with ear and mouth. These *cakras* came to be conceived of as the seat of Male and Female Principles, symbolised by the male and female organs, *liṅga* and *yoni* or *trikoṇa.*[25] The presiding deities of the *cakra* are Tāntric goddesses without any Vedic affiliation.

The theory of letters of the alphabet symbolise different *tattvas* in their qualitatively transformed capacity. It has been held that the letters of the alphabet are the *bīja-mantra* or formula of worship; and in *Tantra*, *mantra* denotes a power (*śakti*) in the form of sound. In the Indian philosophical tradition, sound (*śabda*) is the quality (*guṇa*) of space (*ākāśa*). This sound when unlettered is known as *dhvani* or *dhvanyātmaka-śabda* and when lettered is known as *varṇātmaka-śabda*. By mental action such sounds are co-ordinated into words (*pada*) and sentences (*vākya*) from which a meaning (*artha*) transpires; the mind becomes the subject and the object in the cognitive process (that is, *grāhaka* and *grāhya*), revealer and revealed (*prakāśaka* and *prakāsya*), denoter and denoted (*vācaka* and *vācya*). The mind that thinks of itself as the object of cognition in the form of a deity, is transformed ultimately into the likeness of that deity. This is a fundamental principle of Tāntric *sādhanā*.

*Śabda* has four states (*bhāva*) called *parā*, *paśyanti*, *madhyamā* and *vaikharī*. *Parā* is the motionless casual sound conceived as existing in the *kuṇḍalinī* in the *mūlādhāra-cakra* in a dreamless state of deep sleep (*suṣupati*). *Vaikharī* is the gross sound, the uttered speech by which the ideas are expressed. *Paśyanti* and *madhyamā* are inbetween these two, the former representing a non-particularised motion (*sāmānya-spanda*) and the latter a cognitive aspect of mental movement.[26] Letters as symbols of these forms of sound, are, therefore supposed to exist within the *cakras*. This subtle aspect of the letters is called *mātṛkā*. It is said that consciousness moves as Śakti at first in a subtle form of mind which is in itself the motionless causal sound (*parā-śabda*); then assumes a general undifferentiated movement (*paśyanti sāmānya spanda*); then assumes a differentiated movement (*madhyamā viśeṣa spanda*); and finally, is expressed in a clearly articulated speech (*vaikahrī-spaṣṭatara-spanda*) in the gross form of language as the expression of ideas and of physical objects (*artha*). According to the requirement of the aspirant, gods are produced from *mantras*. Utterance of *mantra* is a preliminary process, not the end.

*Mantra* is unmanifested (*avyakta*) power of sound (*śabda*). This can be awakened and perceived through a variety of practices. The unmanifested power of *śabda* is the cause of the manifested *śabda* and *artha* (words and their meaning). The manifestation is possible through the functioning of *kriyā-śakti*. Every *mantra* is a particular sound form. The sound of alphabets are classified according to the organs used in their articulation (gutteral, palatal, cerebral, dental and labial). When so articulated, each articulated letter touches the *cakra* in which it is. In uttering them, the *cakras* are supposed to react and function. This is the theory put forth to explain the significance of letters in the *cakras*.[27] The *mantras*, because they are lettered and imbued with the aspect of the *mātṛkā*, are eternal and ever effective. Their efficacy does not rest on argument. It is achieved through the realisation of supreme bliss when the *mantra*, its deity and the teachings of the preceptor influence the mind.[28]

*Parā* is the motionless causal sound which produces *nāda* and *vāc*, the uttered speech. The subtle form of these two are, therefore, known *parā nāda* and *parā vāc* and their combination is said to be *parā-śakti*, the source of everything. This *parā-śakti* is same as the *kuṇḍalinī śakti* residing in the *mūlādhāra*. The Śakti of *mūlādhāra* and that of *sahasrāra* are the same in nature; the only difference being that in the former Śakti is latent and in the latter, it is active in the form of consciousness.

Rāghava Bhaṭṭa, the commentator of *Śāradā Tilaka* has stated that this sound element is the nature of consciousness of all beings, known as *vyāpaka-śakti*, *kuṇḍalinī* or *kuṇḍalinī rūpā*, *kāmakalā nāda*, the articulated sound particle in the form of *bindu* (point without space), and it is eventually expressed as Śiva-Śakti equilibrium endowed with all consciousness. In the theory of *mantra*, *nāda* appears in the first stage as a developing, though not yet completely expressed, Śakti and in the second stage as *bindu* and *bīja*, the essential preconditions for the complete manifestation of Śakti. These three, *nāda*, *bindu* and *bīja* are the three angles forming the triangle of the female generative organ.[29] With the help of *mantra*, the *kuṇḍalinī śakti* may be awakened and made to pass through the states of sound-mechanisms like *parā*, *paśyanti*, *madhyamā* and *vaikharī*.[30]

The whole universe with the totality of its phenomena forms one single whole, in which even the smallest element has an effect upon the largest, as secret threads connect the smallest item with the eternal ground of the world.

## References

1. P.C. Bagchi, *Pre-Dravidian and Pre-Aryan in India*, Calcutta, 1929, pp. 10 and 14.
2. *iyam bhumirhi bhūtānām*

   *sāsvati yoniruccate*

   — *Manusmṛti*, IX.33 & 37.

   (N.N. Bhattacharya, *The Indian Mother Goddess*, New Delhi, 1977.)
3. *Ṛgveda*, VII.59.12 (fish); 122.20-21 (*mudrā*); I.152.2 (meat); IV.40.5 (wine); X.184.1-2 (*maithuna*).
4. *Śatapatha Brāhmaṇa*, III.2.1.2; IV.6.7.9-10; V.1.3.10; VI.5.3.5; XI.6.2.10; *Jaiminīya Brāhmaṇa*, II.285, *Kauśitakī Brāhmaṇa*, XV.1.5.
5. *Svetāśvatara Upaniṣad*, 1.1-2: *kuṇḍalinī yoga* is seen in its rudimentary stage in the *Upaniṣad*. The central duct (*nāḍī*) is indirectly referred to in *Chāndogya Upaniṣad* (VI.16). The term *yoga* in its technical sense first occurs in the *Taittirīya Upaniṣad* (11.4) and *Kaṭhopaniṣad* (11.12) as also in *Muṇḍaka Upaniṣad*, 2.6.
6. D.N. Bose and Hira Lal Haldhar, *Tantras, Their Philosophy and Occult Secrets*, Calcutta, 1981, p. 82.
7. In *Vedānta* philosophy, *māyā* is the principle of 'covering'; it is the 'sheath of bliss' (*ānandmaya kośa*), which in the highest depth stays as enveloping the *Brahman*, the ultimate reality. *Brahman* is beyond any concept of will, activity (*ichhā* and

*kriyā*), not will, inactivity or other such positive and negative attributes. It is through the agency of *māyā* as Śakti, Phenomenal Energy as a positive principle of lower order, that this world is projected and brought forth.

8. Gopinath Kaviraj, *Bhāratīya Sanskṛti Aur Sādhanā*, (in Hindi), Patna, 1977, p. 23.

9. S.B. Dasgupta, *Obscure Religious Cults*, Calcutta, 1950, pp. 33 and 34; Nagendra Nath Upadhyay, *Bauddha Kāpālika Sādhanā Aur Sāhitya* (in Hindi), Allahabad, p. 43.

10. Śiva and Śakti stand in the *Tantra* in relation to *prakāśa* and *vimarśa* respectively, the former quality being of nature of pure consciousness, impersonality and inactivity. *Vimarśa* is the spontaneous vibration of the *prakāśa*, the power which gives rise to the world of distinctions but which remains latent in the absolute. The potentiality of the whole object world exists as the *vimarśa* or Śakti. *Prakṛti* or *māyā* is looked upon as the substance of Śakti under whose direction it evolves into the several material elements and physical portions of all sentient beings. Instead of the twenty-five *tattva* of the *Sāṁkhya*, here we have thirty-six classed in *Śaiva tattva* or the absolute, *vidyā tattva* or the subtle manifestation of Śakti and *ātmatattva*, or the material universe from *māyā* down to the earth. The individual under the influence of *māyā* looks upon himself as a free agent and enjoyer, and it is only the knowledge of Śakti that leads to the way of liberation. *Jīvan mukti* or liberation in this life is admitted, which depends on self culture, and on the awakening of forces within the organism. Śiva (*prakāśa*) is subjective illumination, while Śakti (*vimarśa*) is the objective experience. [Gopi Nath Kaviraj, *Tāntrika Vāṅgmaya Aur Śākta-Dṛṣṭi*, (in Hindi), Patna, 1963.]

11. The *Tantra* says that Śiva without Śakti is a lifeless corpse, because wisdom cannot move without power. It is at the same time said that the relation between Śiva, who is the possessor of Śakti and Śakti herself is one of identity; the one cannot be without the other. The attempt to identify Śakti with women is an error. Śiva is said to be the Male Principle and the Śakti is the Female Principle. As a matter of fact, they are neither

male nor female, not are they neuter. The man who worships the power aspect of Reality commonly called the Male Principle, is a Śiva, and he who worships the power aspect or the Female Principle, is called *Śākti*. Śiva as the ruler of universe rides a bull and he rules according to *dharma* (*satya, pavitratā, dayā, dāna*, the *catuṣpada* of *dharma*). When Śiva is worshipped, his consort is also worshipped; for the two are inseparable. Similarly, when Śakti is worshipped Śiva is also worshipped. Other aspects of Śakti are Śrī-Lakṣmī, Durgā, Kālī, Kāmeśvarī, Śivakāmā, Lalitā, Bhuvaneśvarī and Tripurasundarī. [T.N. Misra, Bhāratīya Prācya Sāhitya mein Śiva Kā Svarūpa, *Pariṣad Patrikā*, verṣa 25, aṅk 3, 1985, pp. 72-78.]

12. The man who has realized that truth has no necessity to know the scriptures is just as a man who has tasted nectar to his heart's content and has no necessity for food. The experience of the Ultimate Reality remains as one of the most inexpressible happiness and absolute non-duality. (D.N. Bose, *Tantra, Their Philosophy and Occult Secrets*, Calcutta, 1981, pp. 110-11.)

13. Nagendra Nath Upadhyaya, *Tāntric Bauddha Sādhanā Aur Sāhitya* (in Hindi), Kashi Saṁvat 2015, p. 134; *Śrītattva Cintāmaṇi*, 6 paṭal.

14. *Sakiti Sangam*, 2-22-25 & 3-23-3; *Kulāraṇava*, 5/107-112.

15. *mahim mūlādhārai kamapi maṇipūrai hutābyaham*
*sthitam svādhiṣṭhāni hṛdi marutamā kāśiam purī* ।
*manoapi bhrumadhyai sakalamapibhitvā kulapatim,*
*sahasrārai padmai saharahasi patvā viharasai* ॥
— *Saundarya Laharī*, 9

The Tāntric concept of nerve plexuses situated in different parts of the body and Śakti lying latent as the serpent power to be awakened and sent to its source through these areas by Yogic practices were accepted in theory by Indian religious sects, including the Buddhists and had a wider implication at the cosmic level. In Tāntric monism, the body is divided into two main parts — the head and the trunk as one unit, and the lower body as the other. The centre of the body is inbetween these two, at the base of the spine. The spinal cord represents the earth. The body below this centre is conceived of as being comprised of the several lower or nether worlds and the centre upwards constitutes the seven upper regions marked by six nerve plexuses and the highest cerebral region. These nerve plexuses (known as *cakra, padma*) are related in a particular way to a special machanism of the body through intermediate conductor-nerves (*nāḍīs*). [Bhagawati Prasad Singh, *Maṇīsī Kī Lokayātrā* (in Hindi), Varanasi, 1980, p. 213.]

16. *pañcārai cakra parivartamānai tasminna tasthurbhurāni viśvā* — *Ṛgveda*, 1.164-13; *Svetāśvtara Upaniṣad*, 1.4-6, 6-1.
17. *Ṣaṭcakra Nirūpaṇa*, V.2-13; *Devī Bhāgavat*, XI.1.43; *Mantra Mahodadhi*, IV, 19-25; *Janārṇava*, XXIV, 45-54; *Mahānirvāṇa Tantra*, V.113; *Rudrayāmala*, XXXIV, 6-168.
18. *Ṣaṭcakra Nirūpaṇa*, V.V.14-18.
19. *Ibid.*, V.V.19-21.
20. *Ibid.*, V.V.22-27.
21. *Ibid.*, V.V.28-31.
22. *Ibid.*, V.V.32-38.
23. *Ibid.*; V.V.41-49.
24. *Cakra* is a symbol of the universe (both macrocosm and microcosm) and its divine cause. It has two sets of triangles, one set composed of four male or Śiva triangles, and the other five female (Śakti) triangles. Śakti triangles denote the five *dhātus*, namely, *tvak* (skin), *asrija* (blood), *māṁsa* (flesh), *medā* (fat) and *asthi* (bone) and Śiva triangles denote *majjā* (marrow), *sukra* (vital fluid), *prāṇa* and *jīva*. And from the point of view of the macrocosm, the Śakti triangles stand for the five vital functions, the five senses of knowledge, the five senses of action, the five subtle and five gross forms of matter, and mind, while the Śiva triangles represent the four higher *tattva*, viz., *māyā*, *śuddhavidyā*, Maheśvara and Sadāśiva. In the centre, which is a point (*bindu*), reside Kāmeśvara and Lalitā in *abheda* (undifferentiated) union. Enclosing the *bindu* is an inverted triangle representing the *icchā* (will), *kriyā* (action) and *jñāna* (knowledge) aspects of Śakti; the other *cakra* is *aṣṭakoṇa* (eight pointed).

The divinities of the eight *cakra* from the outermost squares to the innermost triangle are the Śakti of the universe of sound and form, of the objects of experience by the *jīva*, of the means of such experience of the bodily *vṛtti* (functions) and of the mental *vṛtti* (the cognitive modifications of the mind) which are worshipped as but rays emanating from the central luminary, Śrī Lalitā, and are conceived of as being absorbed in Her.

Whether the worship is external, attended with rituals, or internal based upon meditation, emphasis is laid on the *bhāva* (mental certitude) that the Mother withdraws into Herself all the categories that she has projected to create the appearance of the phenomenal world. Now that *sādhaka* has transcended all *vṛtti*, he realizes, in the *bindu cakra*, the Mother Lalitā as the Supreme Essence in whom the static or absolute and dynamic or manifesting aspects coalesce (*prakāśa-vimarśa-parabrahma-svarūpiṇī*) and as the highest bliss (*parāmṛta* Śakti). In the *upāsanā* of *cakra* are harmonized the personal and impersonal aspects of *Brahman*. Ritual and meditation lead to the knowledge of oneness, having gained which one attains Supreme Peace.

25. In the Tāntric religion the female generative organ is seen as a triangle, and in the centre of this triangle is *bindu*, which is known as the male organ. [Gopinath Kaviraj, *Bhāratiya Sanskṛti Aur Sādhanā*, (in Hindi), Patna, 1977, p. 509; Nagendra Nath Upadhyaya, *Tāntric Bauddha Sādhanā Aur Sāhitya*, Kashi, p. 245.]

26. Abhinavaguptacharya, *Sri Tantra Loka*, Part IV, Srinagar (Govt. Publication), 1922.

27. *Navonmeṣa* (M.M. Gopinath Kaviraj, Smriti Granth, in Hindi, Varanasi, 1987, pp. 201 and 220; Bhagavati Prasad Singh, *Maṇīsī Kī Lokayātrā*, in Hindi; M.M. Gopinath Kaviraj, Varanasi, 1980, p. 213.

28. *Śāradātilaka*, 1.55; *Mahānirvāṇa*, 2.18; *Prapañcāsāra*, 1.41; *Paraśurāma Kalpa Sūtra*, 1.11.12.

29. Gopinath Kaviraj, *Bhāratīya Sanskṛti Aur Sādhanā*, (in Hindi), Patna, 1977, pp. 509 and 511 and *Journal of Ganga Nath Jha*

*Research Institute*, Vol. III, Allahabad, pp. 97-108; Nagendra Nath Upadhyaya, *Tāntric Bauddha Sādhanā Aur Sāhitya*, (in Hindi), Kashi Saṁvat 2015, p. 160.

30. *Śāradā Tilaka*, I, 108-11.

# 7

# Tāntric Culture of Buddhism and its Tenets

THE *Tantra* is, in fact, a science dealing with psychic matters, which gives directions for a variety of psychic exercises, requiring competent preceptors and efficient disciples. Like all other sciences, the *Tantra* is not open to all, but only for those who are competent to follow the prescribed practices with patience and zeal. It is the desire of the worshipper, which is of the nature of a psychic force, that reacts on the infinite energy, giving rise to different manifestations according to the nature of the reaction. The nature of this reaction is of illimitable variety, and hence the resultant deity also appears in an infinite variety of forms : this is the chief reason why we find a large number of gods and goddesses in the pantheons of both the Buddhists and the Hindus. The aim of *sādhanā* is the realization of the identity of worshipper and the worshipped, the individual soul and the supreme soul. The concept of *sādhanā* in Tāntrism does not differ in its philosophy from non-Tāntric Buddhist and Hindu philosophy, but is distinct from them in its methods. *Tantra* points to a short-cut route to liberation, making use of psychological aids which help the aspirant to achieve the goal of self-realization quickly. These include *mantra* (incantation), *yantra* (mystic diagrams) *maṇḍala* (circle) *kavaca* (amulets) and *mudrā* (gesture). The aspirant identifies his body with the deity by way of regular practice to finally become the deity. The process of the evolution of the deity is described in Tāntric works. It is mentioned that the form of the deity is an expression of the *śūnya*. Wherever there is an expression, it must be *śūnya* in essence.

In *Hīnayāna* or primitive Buddhism, there was no pantheon of deities. But in *Mahāyāna* a large number of deities was included, and later, in *Vajrayāna* Buddhism, this pantheon became surprisingly large with deities of every description.

Tāntric practices in Buddhism are old. These practices were found in abundance as the references in early Buddhist literature indicate. The attitude of Buddhism seems to have been hostile to such practices but, at the same time, that there were some mystic practices, thought to be harmless, which were tolerated. Buddha is said to have expressed his great disapprobation of *Tantra* or Tāntric practices. He did not permit the consumption of fish, meat, wine and association with the opposite sex in the church, among other things. The result was that even during the lifetime of Buddha, many monks revolted against his injunctions; there were many others who did not openly revolt against the Buddha's injunctions but nevertheless violated them in secret. A result was that there arose secret conclaves of Buddhists who, though professing to be monks, violated all rules of morality and secretly practised what was disapproved by the Buddha and his followers, and disallowed in practice. After the death of Buddha, such secret conclaves must have grown in numbers, till they formed a school of thought in themselves.

It is easy to argue that where Buddhism is concerned, Tāntrism was a natural growth owing to circumstances favourable to this kind of development. Hinduism, too, had a primitive kind of magic in the form of rituals and ceremonies, but these were not practised in secret. The secret Buddhist conclaves that grew on the ruins of the monastic order developed, in course of time, into big organizations known as *Guhyasamāja* which held their teachings and practices in secret (*guhya*). Thus the *Guhyasamāja-tantra* was composed in the *saṅgīti* form (collection of verses). It explained why the teachings of the school were kept secret for so long, and how even a devout Buddhist could practise all that was enjoined in the *tantra*, together with details of theories and practices with rituals. It argued that when Buddha came to the world as Dipāṅkara and Kāśyapa, he did not preach these secret doctrines because people in those days were not found fit to receive such instructions. But it had made the secret doctrines public as the people were prepared to receive such initiation.[1] Its most important declaration was that the emancipation does not depend on bodily sufferings and abstinence from all worldly enjoyments. The work lays down that perfection cannot be obtained through processes which are difficult and painful, but only through the satisfaction of all desires. Its teaching in this respect is direct and unequivocal. In early days, the rules and regulations prescribed for a follower of *Hīnayāna* and *Mahāyāna* were unduly severe, as they brought about much hardship and bodily sufferings. The attainment of Buddhahood was an arduous task that took a long time or even many births. In contrast, *Guhyasamāja* introduced a process by which Buddhahood could be attained within the shortest time possible, and even in a single birth by indulging in all sorts of enjoyment. Another element it introduced in Buddhism was that of Śakti (woman considered as a manifestation of divine energy) for obtaining emancipation through yoga and *samādhi*. The Buddha transformed Himself in the form of 'five *Dhyānī* Buddha' and each of them was associated with a Śakti. Buddhahood was seen as impossible by any means that did not recognise *prajñā* (*vidyā*) or Śakti. The worldly phenomena was actually non-dual in essence though it appeared to be dual.

The Buddhist *Tantra* was divided into four classes for four different types of disciplines — (i) *Caryā Tantra*, (ii) *Kriyā Tantra*, (iii) *Yoga Tantra*, and (iv) *Anuttaryoga Tantra.*[2]

The theory of the 'five *Dhyānī* Buddha' was gradually evolved and it was believed that the 'five *dhyānī* Buddha' — Virocana, Ratnasambhava, Amitābha, Amoghasiddhi and Akṣobhya — presided over the five elements (*skandh*) of which the universe is composed. The elements are form (*rūpa*), ego-consciousness (*vijñāna*), feeling (*vedanā*), perception (*sanjñā*) and impression (*saṁskāra*). The *Dhyānī* Buddha were considered eternal and as manifesting themselves without passing through the intermediate stage of a *Bodhisattva*.

The innovation of the *Dhyānī* Buddha may be considered to be a landmark in the evolution of Tāntric culture among the Buddhists. This was one of the most important theories from which arose the various cults associated with the *Vajrayāna*; and Buddhists were divided according to the relative importance given to one or the other of the *Dhyānī* Buddha. From the *Dhyānī* Buddhas and their Śakti arose their families. The five *Dhyānī* Buddha were considered as nothing but the manifestations of one single power. This power is described as the embodiment of *śūnya* or *vajra*, from which the name of the school *Vajrayāna* is derived. One who embodies the *vajra*, *vajrasattva*, does not feel himself bound by any laws, social or otherwise, which are mostly the creations of imperfect beings. He is one with the Ultimate Reality that creates, maintains and destroys everything, and views the imperfect world from the standpoint of the *śūnya*, or the ultimate creative energy.

This concept was woven into all forms of Tāntrism, which were termed, in general, as *Vajrayāna* or the *Vajra-path* to salvation. It was called *Vajrayāna* because *śūnya* came to be designated by the term *vajra* on accounts of its indestructibility. The *śūnya* of the *Vajrayāna* is something different from the *śūnya* of the *Mādhyamikas* (nihilists) or the *Vijñānavādins* (idealists), because it includes the three elements, *śūnya* (reality), *vijñāna* (consciousness) and *mahāsukha* (great bliss). The *Vajrayāna* attracted many and it made many contributions to Buddhism and Buddhist culture in general.

*Vajrayāna* also gave rise to several *yānas* (paths) i.e., *Sahajayāna, Kālacakrayāna* and *Mantrayāna. Sahajayāna* teachings held that no suffering, fasting, rites, purification or obedience to the rules of society are necessary for the purpose of obtaining emancipation; it is not necessary to bow down before the images of gods which are made of wood, stone, metal or mud. But the worshipper should, with concentration, offer worship only to his own body where all gods reside.

The *Kālacakrayāna* seems to be a later development of the *Vajrayāna.* It concerns itself with the *yoga tantra* and *anuttarayoga tantra* and incorporates the doctrines of the *Sahajayāna* also. According to *Kālacakra Tantra, Kālacakra* is a deity and an embodiment of *śūnyatā* and *karuṇā* (compassion), is embraced by the goddess *Prajñā,* and represents the philosophical conception of *advaya* or non-duality. He is regarded as the *Ādibuddha* (the progenitor even of the Buddha), that is to say, the *Dhyānī* Buddha. One's own body, in which the whole world is manifest, has a resemblance to the doctrines of the *Sahajayāna* and Nāthism, and this makes it probable that the *Kālacakrayāna* is embodied in the teachings of the *Vajrayāna, Sahajayāna* and Nāthism.

The *Mantrayāna* concerns itself with *mantra* and *yantra.* It believes that certain special mystic forces are generated by reciting words in a certain manner and they can help one to obtain whatever one desires including emancipation.

All the important Tāntric sects had one common goal: the attainment of non-duality (*advaya*), also called *sahaja* or *kaula,* the state in which all dualistic knowledge disappears and the *sādhaka* becomes identical with the object of his devotion. For attaining this aim different sects advocated different means ranging from the sexo-yogic techniques of arousing *kuṇḍalinī* to *aghorī* practices. The *Sahajiyās* (both Hindu and Buddhist) were averse to the method of knowing the truth through discursive reason and were not in favour of meditation and *mantra*. They protested against the formalities of life and religion and accepted human nature as the best help for realizing the truth. Sexual orgies were practised by the Kaulas and Kāpālikas. Attainment of salvation meant becoming like Śiva, Buddha and Alakhanirañjana. The Buddhist *Sahajiyā* and *Nātha-panthī* believed in *bindu-siddhi* or yogic control of semen (*vīrya*) during the sexual act and gave much attention to the *vāmācāra* rites including *cakra-pūjā*, the worship of a living beautiful woman, and the practice of a secret form of intercourse where there was no distinction of caste. Thus, it seems that the serious intent in the rigorous path of Tāntric *sādhanā* was lost, leaving behind the belief that only the pursuit of pleasure ultimately led to *mokṣa*.

With the influential concept of Śāktism, the primitive Tāntric rituals, basically sexual in character, made their way into different kinds of religious systems as the highly technical and sophisticated culture of the five *ma-kāra*. The woman, flesh and sexual intercourse came to be regarded as essential preconditions for attainment of liberation. The idea of *yuganaddha* (god in sexual union with the goddess), an iconological form by which the Buddha and Bodhisattva were frequently represented, shows the extent to which the Buddhists were influenced by the Tāntric way of life. The central theme of the two basic works on Tāntric Buddhism deals with the *mudrās* and *maṇḍalas* who are connected with goddesses and spirititually oriented women who can come from any class of people. The aspirant has to understand that the woman or her generative organ is the source of existence and that sexual functioning is the imitation of the process of creation.

According to the Tāntric view the act of creation is due to the union of the Female and Male Principles, the former being the more important functionary. In Buddhist *tantra* these two principles are known as *prajñā* and *upāya* or as *śūnya* and *karuṇā* (also called *lalanā* and *rasanā*) respectively. The union of *prajñā* and *upāya* is *yuganaddha* or *samarasa*. One who can unite these two principles in oneself can have the highest knowledge and supreme bliss, and become free from the fetters of birth and death. This is the real Buddhahood. In order to have this spiritual experience, man and woman should first realise that they are representative of *upāya* and *prajñā* respectively and that their physical, mental and intellectual union alone can bring the experience of the highest truth.[3] Accordingly, men and women should jointly strive for this secret knowledge. *Prajñā* is the Female Principle and as such she is Bhagavatī or the goddess herself. She is known as *vajra kanyā* and *yuvatī*. The woman who is to impersonate *prajñā* should preferably be a beautiful maiden. *Prajñā* also denotes the female organ which is the seat of all happiness, also known as *Sukhāvatī*. *Upāya*, the Male Principle, is known as *vajra*, which means the male generative organ. The union of man and woman, of *prajñā* and *upāya*, bring the maximum pleasure in which all mental action is lost and the world around forgotten; only a pleasing experience of non-duality prevails.[4] This is known as the greatest pleasure (*mahāsukha*) or *nirvāṇa*, the *summum-bonum* and real manifestation of *bodhicitta*.[5]

This *sahaja* bliss (*mahāsukha*) is not to be misunderstood as gross sex pleasure. It is the subtlest and the highest state of becoming that could only be reached by experiencing distinct stages (moments) of bliss in an ascending order. It demarcates the *cakras* or centres of consciousness at different plane or levels of anthropomorphic personality. The *cakras* along with their particular 'flavour' of joys transform the individual personality stage-by-stage into cosmic existence or selfless immortality.

Buddhist *Tantras* speak of three nerve cycles symbolising the three bodies of *Buddha* — *dharma*, *saṁbhoga* and *rūpa* or *nirmāṇa*; an additional nerve cycle is *uṣṇīśa kamala* in the central region which is the symbol of the Buddha's *vajra-kāya* or *sahaja-kāya* and which corresponds to the *Śākta* concept of *sahasrāra*. Below this, around the neck is *saṁbhoga-cakra*, near the heart *dhama-cakra* and near the naval, *nirmāṇa-cakra*. There are innumerable nerves within the body. Of these three are most important : two symbolising *prajñā* and *upāya* are on either side of the spinal cord, and the third is known as *sahaja* or *avadhūti*. Like the *kuṇḍalinī-Śakti* of the *Śākta Tantras*, the Buddhist *Tantra* speak of a female energy having the force of fire which resides in *nirmāṇa-cakra* and is known as *candāli*. This *candāli* being accelerated, it kindles the *dharma* and *saṁbhoga-cakra* and ultimately reaches the *uṣṇīśa-kamala*, the highest cerebral region and then returns to its own place.[6]

The union of *prajñā* and *upāya* through the principle of *yuganaddha* for the purpose of the realisation of the non-dual state, symbolised by the physical union of the adept and his female partner, brings in succession *rāga* and *mahārāga* (emotion and intense emotion, evidently transcendental, resulting from a genuine feeling of compassion) *samarasa* (oneness of emotion) in which there is no cognition of *prajñā* and *upāya*, and finally the *mahāsukha* or great bliss which is of the nature of the absolute unity of *prajñā* and *upāya*, the non-dual quintessence of all the entities without which perfect wisdom is never possible.

## Sahajīya Buddhism and its Sādhanā

After the demise of Lord Buddha, the spirit of revolution, which served as the very kernel of all Buddhistic thought and religion, faded as a result of slow but continued friction with Hindu thoughts and practices. As a result, there seems to have developed a spirit of compromise by way of which the concept of Tāntrism entered Buddhism, giving rise to a composite religion known as Tāntric Buddhism or Sahajīya Buddhism. Sahajīya Buddhists developed a theology of their own which is substantially different from the philosophy and religion of canonical Buddhism.

According to the Sahajīya Buddhist, *Bodhicitta* is the highest truth; it is the Absolute. It is the *sahaja*, the innate nature of the self and the world. This *bodhicitta* is explained as a unified state of *śūnyatā* (void) and *karuṇā* (universal compassion). *Śūnyatā* is a perfect knowledge of the lack of essence in all that is and is not — it is a perfect wisdom (*prajñā*). This *prajñā* is the static or passive aspect of Reality. *Karuṇā*, or the strong emotion of compassion, is the dynamic principle that leads one to an active life for the liberation of not only the self, but also of others; it is therefore the active principle and is called the *upāya* (the means). *Prajñā* as a pure consciousness or as pure wisdom represents the domain of *nivṛtti*, while *upāya*, as the active principle, represents the domain of *pravṛtti*. The *prajñā* and *upāya* stand in esoteric Buddhism for the same principles as Śiva and Śakti in Hindu *Tantras*, the only difference being that unlike Hinduism, the passive principle is taken here to be the goddess (woman), while the active principle is the Lord (man).

This esoteric yogic school of Buddhism held, as is consistent with the spirit of *Tantras*, that the body is the abode of truth and at the same time, the best instrument or medium for realizing the truth. With this belief it located in it four plexuses (lotuses or *cakras*) in different parts of the body along the spinal column. The first is the *nirmāṇa-cakra* (*maṇipūraka cakra*) situated in the naval region, representing the *nirmāṇa-kāya* or the principle of material transformation; the second is *dharma-cakra* (*anāhata-cakra*) situated in the cardiac region, representing the *dharma-kāya* or the principle of non-dual cosmic existence; and the third is the *saṁbhoga-cakra* (*viśuddha-cakra*) situated near the neck, representing the *saṁbhoga-kāya* or the principle of the body of Bliss. Above all these and transcending all these is the lotus (plexus) in the head called *uṣṇīśa kamala* (*sahasrāra*) which is the seat of Absolute Truth. The cosmic energy or feminine principle remains as a fierce fire-force (*candālī*) in the *nirmāṇa-cakra*,[7] and here, associated with all gross principles of defilement, she acts as the principle of phenomenalism. She must be roused and dissociated from all principles of defilement and given an upward motion, so as to reach the *uṣṇīṣa kamala*, which is the region of perfect rest and purity. The important nerve on the left side of the body, called the Moon or the River Gaṅgā, represents *prajñā* or the Woman and the nerve on the right side, called Sun (Sūrya) of the River Yamunā, represents the *upāya* or the Man, the Lord (the ovum being the symbol for the Goddess and seed for the Lord). The left and right should be controlled and commingled in such a way that all their functions (including flow of the vital current), *prāṇa* and *apāna* being the two nerves, may be completely unified in the middle path called the *avadhūti*, and such perfect union results, ultimately, in the realization of Infinite Bliss (*mahāsukha*), which is the quintessence of the *bodhicitta*. Again, *prajñā* manifests herself in every woman, and every man is the embodiment of *upāya*.

In the actual *sādhanā*, the man and woman must first of all transcend their corporeal existence and realize their true self as *upāya* and *prajñā* respectively. With such a realization they should unite and control the sex act in such a way that the downward motion of the seed may be arrested and an upward motion given to it till it reaches the highest plexus and remains there motionless. This motionless state of the seed in the highest plexus conduces to infinite bliss and tranquillity, and realization of the highest bliss is realization of the highest truth, for bliss is the ultimate nature of truth. *Prajñopāya* (*prajña* and *upāya*) is, therefore, equivalent to *mahāsukha* (supreme bliss) and entirely auspicious (*sāmantabhadra*). The state of perfection is neither duality nor non-duality. Wisdom conceived as the female is to be combined in one's own self for the purpose of liberation which is perfect enlightenment through the practical experience of the

Female Principle. *Prajñā* or wisdom is linked with a state of intense emotion called *sukha* (bliss) or *mahāsukha* (or great bliss) which is conducive to complete enlightenment. *Prajñā* is often identified in flesh and blood — a woman, and the concept of *mahāsukha* is sought to be explained in terms of sexual symbolism, which is in general agreement with the common Tāntric tradition. The highest state of the union of the two is that of supreme love and it is the real *sahaja-mahā-sukha*. This love may be conjugal (*svakīya*) but it should be perfectly unconventional (*parakīya*).

The final aim in all such cases was the attainment of an infinitely blissful state of arrest (*samādhi*), either purely through a psycho-physiological process of *yoga* or through the absorbing emotion of love, strictly disciplined and intensified through practice of *yoga*. Intense human love, or sexual pleasure, thus transformed beyond recognition, has the capacity to produce a supreme state of arrest. In a unique flow of intensely blissful realization, uninterrupted by the notions of subjectivity and objectivity, there dawns an infinite oneness in the mind, which is said to be the state of unity of emotion (*samarasa*). All the subjective and objective disturbances of the mind are absolutely lost in a supreme realization of Bliss and in that state we attain our true self, which is *sahaja*. To judge this state of *samarasa* or *sahaja* as a pure state of *samādhi*, a *sādhaka* practises *yoga* in the plane of mind (*citta-bhūmi*).

What actually happened, however, was that neither a suitable teacher (*guru*) was available nor an adept underwent through the preliminary course of training. Such non-observation of the conditions prescribed in *Tantra*, inevitably led to abuses. One may conclude by saying that in no religion or a sect thereof have the promulgators in no religion given scope to such abuses as did the earliest of the Vajrayāna Buddhists.

## References


1. *Indian Historical Quarterly*, March, 1933, p. 5.
2. S.B. Dasgupta, *An Introduction to Tantric Buddhism*, Calcutta, 1974, pp. 64 onwards.
3. Alex Wayman, "Female Energy and Symbolism in the Buddhist Tantra", in *History of Religion*, Vol. II, No. 1, 1962, p. 80.
4. The highest mortal joy that ensues from the coital act is only momentary or ephemeral with the discharge of semen; its normal downward flow when checked and reversed by the *yogi* towards the seat of consciousness in the lotus — the 'return of semen' — marks the emanation of the Supreme Bliss that is permanent and the cause of immortality. Thus it is *śukram* or 'semen virile' that is sometimes described as the Supreme Bliss. In the *Hevajra Tantra*, the Lord Buddha himself says 'I am existence, I am not existence. I am the Enlightened One for I am enlightened about what things are. My nature is that of *sahaja* bliss and I come at the end of joy of cessation (*virāma-ānanda*). I am the Lord with thirty-two marks, the Lord with eighty characteristics. I dwell in the Sukhāvati of the *bhaga* (vagina) of women and my form is *śukram* (semen) — without that (i.e., *śukram*) there is no bliss and without bliss this would not be. Since one can never be effective without the other, bliss ensues only in union with female divinity. [*Hevajra Tantra* ed. & tr. by D.L. Snellgrove, London, 1959, Vol. I and II (pp. 48-50).]
5. *Yuganaddha* is also described as the non-dual state and identified with the *Bodhicitta*, and defined as a state of absolute non-duality marked by the absence of notions like worldly process and cessation of that process (*nivṛtti*), adherance (*saṅkleśa*) and distinction (*vyavadhāna*), perceivable and perceiver (*grāhya* and *grāhaka*). [H.V. Gunther, *Yuganaddha*, Benaras, 1952.]
6. S.B. Dasgupta, *An Introduction to Tantric Buddhism*, Calcutta, 1974, pp. 77.
7. Nagendra Nath Upadhyaya, *Tāntric Bauddha Sādhanā Aur Sāhitya*, Kashi, Saṁvat, 2015, pp. 12 to 14.

## 8

# Siddhi, Siddha and the Nātha Cult

THE idea of a supernatural power (*siddhi*) is universal in the ancient Indian religious systems. Almost all sects attach great importance to *yoga* in some form or other. The *siddhi* is also known as *ṛddhi*. A *siddha* is one who possesses these powers. The great human teachers who had attained powers through the practice of *yoga*, according to theory, were eighty-four *siddhas*. All *siddhas* are historical personages and authors of works on their special *sādhanā* (spiritual practice). The general trend of teaching was esoteric and a qualified teacher (preceptor) was allowed to initiate the disciple in the mysteries. These teachers (*gurus*) were also known as *siddhācāryas*. In this *panth* (cult), the *guru* (*siddhācārya*) was given the exalted position. The truth that is free from duality was taught by the *guru* and it was believed that nothing was unattainable by him whom the teacher favoured.

What was the *sādhanā* in which the *guru* had to initiate his disciple? This *sādhanā* involved the practice of a new form of *Yoga*, which evolved in the hands of the *siddhācārya*. The Tāntric *yoga* does not go against Nature; it follows the law of nature, which is by itself inclined to move towards self-realisation. According to Tāntric *yoga*, the *sādhaka* should have a positive attitude towards life and the world. Having a positive attitude means two things, First, it means accepting the worldly desires and objects of enjoyment (*bhoga*), and treating them in such a way as to move towards sublimation. Secondly, it means having the attitude that everything of the world is divine. Hence, we cannot kill the desires; we can only transform or sublimate them. This is the reason why *Tantra* advocates the *sādhanā* of *kaula-mārga* or *vāma-mārga*. The basic desires (sex-desire) are accepted in the *Tantra* as currents of energy originating from one and the same basic source, *cit-śakti* or *kuṇḍalinī*. The *Tantra* aims at controlling and regulating these currents so that they flow through sublime channels and yield better results.

According to Hindu *Tantra* and Buddhist *Tantra*, there are thirty-two *nāḍīs* (nerve-channels) within the body.[1] The energy, which has its seat below the naval, flows up into the head through these channels. The topmost is called *mahāsukha sthāna* (the place of great bliss). The topmost station is imagined to be a lotus having either sixty-four or thousand petals. Various names are given to the nerve-channels, and among them the *lalanā*, *rasanā* and *avadhūti* are the most important for they combine in themselves, at particular stations, the currents supplied by the rest. The *avadhūti* is the middlemost channel and corresponds to the *suṣumnā* of the Hindu *Tantra*, while the other two correspond to the *iḍā* and *piṅgalā*. There are also a number of stations, compared to lotuses (wheel-*cakras*)[2] within the body, and psychic energy in its upward march has to pass through them. The ultimate goal is the creation of the stage of *sahaja* which is one of great bliss. It is a state which is without beginning and without end, a state which is free from duality. When this state is attained, the objective world disappears from view and all the aggregates, elements and senses merge in it. The *sādhaka* then finds himself to be the sole reality, identical with the universe and with the Buddha (a being who is ever free).

*Siddhas* believe that the body is the microcosm of the universe; mountain, sea, moon, sun and river—all that which the world is composed of are within the human body. It is by *Haṭhayoga* that one is able to have total control over the body and mind; so they believe in *kāya-sādhanā*. Śiva and Śakti reside in the body, the former in the *mahāsukha sthāna* (*sahasrāra*) which is in the highest cerebral region, and the latter in the *mūlādhāra*, the lowest extremity of the spinal cord. The right half of the body is Śiva and the left half, Śakti. Through the nerve *piṅgalā* in the right flows the *apāna* wind which is the stream of Śiva. Likewise through the nerve *iḍā* flows the *prāṇa* wind which is the stream of Śakti. The aspirant, through yogic efforts, has to bring these two streams into the middle nerve which is *suṣumnā*. If this is achieved there will be a perfect equilibrium of Śiva and Śakti within the body. Again, male is the symbol of Śiva and female that of Śakti and the yogic union is supposed to be the cause of *mahāsukha* (great bliss), arising when one experiences absolute non-duality. If one can realise the truth of the body (*bhāṇḍa*), one can also realise the truth of the universe (*brahmāṇḍa*).

The esoteric cult professed by the Kanaphaṭa Yogī wearing *kuṇḍala* is known as the *Nātha* cult. The *Nātha* cult is a *Śaiva* cult, which uses *rudrākṣa*, i.e., rosaries and *tripuṇḍra* of ash on the forehead. Śivarātri is the major festival of this cult. *Vaiṣṇava* association, Buddhist affiliation, and association with Jain and other sects as well are woven into the complex texture of the *Nātha* cult. *Śākta* elements are also accepted in this cult. *Nātha* cult was never seriously theistic. The Supreme Being was referred to by the epithets of *nirañjana* (speckless), *śūnya* (void), *anādi* (that which has no beginning) and *ādinātha* (primal lord).[3] This cult also came to be mixed up with similar yogic and Tāntric cults which did not strictly forbid contact with women.[4]

The aim of the esoteric practices of the cult was the attainment of the state of neutrality (*sahaja*), where there is no birth and death as such. According to the philosophy of the cult, existence and extinction are results of man's desire and cogitation; his fetters and mode of release are of his own creation as well. A true *yogī* moves beyond the world of thought; to him activity (*karma*) has no appeal, and salvation (*nirvāṇa*) is meaningless. For the attainment of the state of neutrality, the *yogī*, following the instructions of his *guru* (spiritual teacher), has to check the downward movement of the semen, hold up the truth, and stabilize the mind. These processes are known as *bindu-dhāraṇa*, *citta nirodha* and *pavananiścāñcalya*.[5]

This school is based on the belief of thc two aspects of the Absolute Reality, represented by the Sun (sūrya) and the Moon (candra). The sun stands for the principle of destruction (*kālāgni*), through the process of death and decay, and the moon stands for the principle of immutability. The final aim of *Nātha siddhas* is the attainment of the non-dual state, through the attainment of immortality, in a perfect and divine body. This non-dual state of immortality, which is the state of the Maheśvara (Great Lord), can be attained only through the union, rather the commingling, of the sun and the moon.

The main *sādhanā* of the *Nātha siddhas* had to do with culturing the body (*kāya-sādhanā*), implying transubstantiation of the body first into a subtle ethereal body and then, finally, into an immutable divine body having an eternal existence. The moon, which is the depository of *soma* or *amṛta* (nectar), is situated just below the *sahasrāra*, the lotus of thousand petals. The quintessence of the visible body is distilled in the form of *soma* in the moon; this *soma* rejuvenates the body and makes it immortal. In the ordinary course, this *soma* trickles down from the moon above and is dried up by the sun, the fire of destruction, situated in the naval plexus; this drying up of the *soma* by the sun leads ordinary beings to decay and death. This *soma* (also known as *mahārasa*, the great juice) must be protected from the sun.

According to Nāthism, the Ultimate Reality has two aspects which are symbolised by the sun and moon. While the sun is *kālāgni*, the principle of death and destruction, the moon, on the other hand, is the symbol of unchangeability. The aim of a *Nātha* aspirant is to feel within his own self the ideal of non-duality which is possible by the attainment of immortality and the renovation of the body; generally Śiva represents this non-dual state, and its attainment is possible by connecting the forces of the Sun and Moon within the body. The essence which helps the human body to survive is produced from the *soma*, identified also as the moon, which is the source of the drug of immortality (*amṛta*) and which is found in the *sahasrāra* or the cerebral region of the body. If it is properly utilised one can attain immortality. But there is a difficulty in that the *amṛta* dropped from *soma* or the moon is consumed by the sun which resides in the naval region. However, there is a serpent-like channel within the body having two faces known as *baṅka-nāla* or *śaṅkhinī*, and the face from which the *amṛta* drops — known as the tenth-door (*daśa-dvāra*).[6] The door can be closed and this is possible or achieved only by *kāya-sādhanā* (the disciplining of the body).[7] The Hara-Gaurī conception of Nāthism is an adaptation of both the Mahāyānic *karuṇā* and *śūnyatā*, and Vajrayānic *upāya* and *prajñā*. Nāthism believes in three kinds of *śūnya* — *ādi śūnya*, *madhya śūnya* and *antaḥ śūnya* (the *śūnyavāda* of the *Mādhyamika* system is also accepted in Nāthism). The *śūnya* is to be realised through *yoga*. By the yogic control of breath, the thirty knots in the spinal cord can be loosened, as a result of which the two vital winds, *prāṇa* and *apāna*, can enter the spinal cord and move upwards as *haṁsa* through the six nerve plexuses — *mūlādhāra*, *svādhiṣṭhāna*, *maṇipūraka*, *anāhata*, *viśuddha* and *ājñā* — and on reaching the *sahasrāra* region, assume the nature of *śūnya*. There are 7200 nerves within the body of which sixty-four can be distinctly located and fifteen utilised for yogic purposes.

It has already been stated that the *amṛta* or the essence which flows from the moon within the body is consumed by the sun. The former is the creative principle and the latter, the destructive principle. These two principles are understood to stand for the right and left nerve channels respectively. According to another conception the moon is Śiva and the sun is Śakti, representing man and woman respectively. The moon being the source of creation and preservation, it is supposed to have the *amṛta* which the sun (Śakti or women) is eager to consume and that is why women should be avoided.

## References

1. S.B. Dasgupta, *An Introduction to Tantric Buddhism*, Calcutta, 1974, pp. 153-54.
2. In the *Ṛgveda*, the word *cakra* is used with reference to Sūrya (Sun) and the Earth, and the human body is defined or compared with *cakra*. 1.164-11 and 1.164-13; *Atharvaveda*, 9.9.1 and 9.9.2, 9.9.11, *Kaṭhopaniṣad*, 1.3.3.
3. The Nātha *siddhas* believe that Ādinātha was the first *Nātha*, the founder of all esoteric science. He is very often equated with Śiva and *Vajrasattva*.

   G.W. Briggs, *Gorakhnath and the Kanphata Yogis*, Calcutta, 1938.
4. Hazari Prasad Dwivedi, *Nāth Sampradāya*, (in Hindi), Allahabad, 1950, pp. 86-88.
5. *Maraṇam bindupātena jīvanam bindu dhāraṇāt.* In Buddhist Tāntrism the semen called *Bodhicitta* (the name of Bodhicitta given to semen) implies the generation of the spiritual message of the Master, who was in favour of celibacy. It was also believed in the later stage of Buddhism that 'Buddhahood lies in the female generative organ' or *bīja* is not to be cast. The fall of the semen is considered a great sin. The semen must not be emitted, for otherwise the *yogīn* falls under the Law of Time and Death. For checking the flow of semen, the *sādhaka* practises coitus reservatus by taking recourse to *Haṭha-Yoga* or the psychophysical technique. The semen instead of flowing downwards is led by *yoga* to the highest centre of the body or the *uṣṇīśa kamala* of Buddhist *Tantra* or *Sahasrāra cakra* of Hindu *Tantra*. [Nagendra Nath Upadhyaya, *Tantric Bauddha Sādhanā Aur Sāhitya*, Kashi, Saṁvat, 2015, pp. 3-15; *Haṭhayogapradīpikā*, tr. by Pancham Singh, Allahabad, 1915, (III, 83-88).]
6. *Svetāśvatara Upaniṣad*, 3.18.
7. S.B. Dasgupta, *Obscure Religious Cults*, Calcutta, 1950, pp. 211-55.

# 9

# Influence of Tantra in Art

INDIAN art, in one sense, could be seen as a combination of the abstract philosophical concepts of Āryan origin and the representational, even naturalistic trends, of the Dravidian. Indian art may also be described as theological and traditional where tradition may mean a kind of healthy discipline conditioned by belief and prescriptions, which embrace the whole of a civilization in all its modes and trends. The purpose of Indian art has been to communicate the great truths to mankind through architectural, sculptural and pictorial reconstructions of the power that maintains the stars in their courses. Thus, in a way, every Indian religious structure and art form may be regarded as a replica of an unseen celestial region or as a cosmos in itself. Indian art depicts life as interpreted by religion and philosophy. The religious texts specifically state that the making of images leads to heaven. Ancient Indian art, in all periods of development, was closely associated with the rhythm of life including the life of the gods and all living beings on earth. The Indian tradition interprets the living world as a manifestation of god. The symbols of art voice the same truth as our philosophy and myths. The *Vedas* and early *Brāhmaṇa* had practically nothing to say on such topics as the 'law of *karma*', the transmigration of soul and its necessary concomitant. Thus, the Vedic people may have held a somewhat pessimistic view of life. But the points were gradually discussed more and more in the *Upaniṣads*.

*Bhakti* (devotion)[1] denotes primarily the loving adoration of some persons by others, but secondarily, the deeply affectionate and mystic devotion for some personal deity who is the object of worship (*pūjā*). There was the belief in one's personal god as the spiritual being, the faith that his power is sufficient to secure and the good will prevails, and the conception of the nexus that binds together God and worshippers. The image or icon, or any such visible symbol of his deity was the medium through which a devotee could transfer his one-souled devotion to his god. The rendering of one's homage was done by various acts of *pūjā* (worship) in which images became obvious and came to be seen as absolutely necessary; the act of *pūjā* thus, has a special bearing on the history of the evolution of the icons. The origin of image worship in India can be traced to very early times and the circumstances behind such a development are not exactly known. The image worship was probably not unknown to the Vedic peoples but the religion of the *Veda*s knew no idol worship.

In the Hindu religious thought, the omnipresent God, who is the creator of the universe, is said to reside in everything and as much of his presence is felt in the loving heart of a devotee as in stocks and stones. His God may or may not be conceived as anthropomorphic; the form of the conception depends upon the stage of advancement of the worshipper *vis-a-vis* divine knowledge and spiritual wisdom. To a *sādhaka*, who realises the presence of the supreme *Brahman* within himself, there is hardly any need of a temple or a divine image of worship. But to those who cannot attain this kind of realisation, various modes of mental and physical exercises are prescribed. The images of the Hindu gods and goddesses are representations meant for those who cannot realise the divine spirit in their hearts. The thoughts of thinkers, made manifest and concretised by various means, such as speech, pictorial and sculptural representations, signs and symbols, have helped in evolving divine images. In its metaphysical essence, the formless undergoes a definite mode of cosmic operation. It arises from certain movements of the life-force that animates all matter, and by a process of expansion and growth or of condensation and construction causes it to crystallize uncertain shapes. These, as its outer limiting circumscription, show the nature of its formation (*dhyāna-rūpa*). Lines, forms and colours are not accidental, but are direct manifestations of these inner forces related to the spiritual reality. All these means have been utilised to depict divinity at the level of the common man in order to lift him up gradually to the sublime height of true realisation.

The *bhakti* cult gave a significant impetus to the construction of images and houses of gods. Vaiṣṇavism refers to the theistic religion of which Viṣṇu is the object of worship and devotion as the Supreme God. *Bhakti* or emotional attachment to God was considered as a road to *mokṣa* (salvation) — the easiest one and a path open to all. *Bhakti* (devotion) popularised image worship, as meditation on the unmanifested Absolute was considered a difficult process.

Although the *Jains* denied the existence of a Supreme Being, they recognised the practice of worshipping images of their *Tīrthāṅkaras*. Where the history of image-worship in the Buddhist tradition is concerned, during the first century AD, the liberal Mahāsāṅghikas and then the Mahāyānists paved the way for devotees to erect the Buddha images for expressing their devotion, probably to satisfy the religious emotions of the people. The figure of *Bodhisattva* (who is required to acquire certain *pāramitās* and qualify himself for the attainment of Buddhahood) was the first to be introduced. This was probably due to the fact that the Master (Buddha) was basically a Teacher, and not a saviour god, and those who were orthodox were anxious to avoid any form of worship while harding the Buddha's relics in reverence. But the convention was shortly to disappear. Iconographic types of Buddha made their appearance in art with the Indian conception of a great man (*mahāpuruṣa lakṣaṇas*). Another concept of Buddhism that finds its reflection in the iconography is the three bodies of Buddha. This three-fold division was of a philosophical nature and was designated as *dharma-kāya* (word of Buddha), *saṁbhoga-kāya* (body of bliss) and *nirmāṇa-kāya* (noumenal body). A further development was the creation of mystical Buddhas for the four direction and one for the centre of the world — the group of Buddhas of this theory is called the five *Dhyānī* Buddhas. The last phase of the religious salvation was offered through Tāntric worship, which essentially meant devotion paid to the female energy of Śakti, which in its grosser aspects encouraged sexual practices as a means of salvation.

The art of sculpture and painting attained a state of perfection in ancient India that could stand comparison with what was attained in other countries. The Indian artist was not wanting in originality and vigour in the handling of his subjects. He was also true to nature and in the representation of birds and animals he remained often unsurpassed. In the early period of the history of Indian art, the imagination of the artist was not tied down by any religion prescription which, however, became the bane of art in later time. An early factor that brought about a change in this natural and progressive state of Indian art was the introduction of Tāntric ideas in the worship of the Hindus as well as the Buddhists. One of the characteristic features of Indian art and architecture is the quality it derives from using motifs rich in symbolism and mythical imagery. *Maithunas*, for instance, which appeared in early Indian terricottas and the *dvāraśākhās* of the Gupta temples, were imageries that lent a special beauty to Indian architecture when translated into stone. We may also note that very few specimens of Indian art have offered such a fruitful source of comment and controversy as have the erotic sculptures of Konark and Khajuraho. Here we have generic couples trying to convey some kind of masonic symbolism, the meaning of which we shall endeavour to discover.

Now we shall discuss, specifically, the influence of the erotic and the impact of Tāntrism in art. We will begin with a reference to the cult of Śiva. The cult of Śiva goes back to very early times (some trace it even to the pre-Vedic period as Śiva represented as Paśupati and depictions his emblem *par excellence* the *Śiva-linga* (the phallic emblem of Śiva), according to them, have been found in the remains of the Indus Valley Civilization). Whatever may be his origin, he attained his characteristics from the Vedic Rudra and gradually rose to prominence. It appears that from the very early times, certain mystic practices were associated with the *pāśupata* religion. When inelligible persons began to adopt them, considerable deterioration set in and the system itself fell into disrepute. But it is to be remembered that any mystic cult can be distorted and can become vitiated by left-handed practices (*vāmācāra*). It is presumable that human as well as phallic forms of the god were at first enshrined in the main sanctum of the *Śaiva* temples. It became the general custom afterwards to place *Śiva-liṅgas* only in it and use them as the principal object of worship, the human figures of Śiva being present in the reliefs in various parts of the temples.

Archaeological materials from the Indus Valley Civilization also point to the existence of a fertility cult in India from the protohistoric period. The discovery of numerous phallic stones and ring stones, the figure of a male ithyphallic horned god (probably the prototype of Śiva) and the figure of a Mother Goddess are ample to indicate the prevalence of the said cults.[2] However, no representation of the sexual act has been reported in the art and ritual objects yielded by the Indus Civilization. The earliest depiction of the sexual act among the objects excavated so far in India, is found on a pot of the chalcolithic period at Dāimābād.[3] Another early representation of sex has been noted in the Kupgallu cave in Mysore.[4] Significant material on the possible connection of the depiction of erotic couples with fertility cults is available in the historical period.[5] The secular subjects drawn from everyday life were introduced in the art of terracotta and in the stone monuments also. The religious theme gradually received an artistic treatment, with the result that it turned into an art motif. The process of secularization and sensualization of ritual or cultic objects is clearly noticeable in the ivory figure of Śrī found at Ter that has been assigned to the second century AD. Śrī was a goddess of abundance, fertility, blissful prosperity, luck and beauty. Her fertility aspects are revealed in *Śrī-Sūkṭa*, a *Khila* of *Ṛgveda*.

The cults of fertility (specially the cults of goddess Śrī) have a direct bearing on the depiction of *maithunas* in religious art. All important religious sects of the country — Hindu, Jain and Buddhist — presented erotic motifs in their art. Sexual representation was a pan-Indian cultural feature. It implies a common cultural substratum which influenced religious sects all over India. This common substratum is seen in those beliefs and practices which show the primal connection between sex and religion. Far from being suppressed, sex played an important part in the religious life of early communities and civilizations. It was realized that it was necessary to experiment in art before conventionalizing the aspects in texts — like the *śilpa*-canons. Forms, once accepted in art, have a tendency to become conventionalized and assume the character of motifs. In the culture of India which glorifies traditional values, the process of conventionalization became a major factor leading to persistence and inertia in the use of motifs.

The religious structures were the means to express the above-mentioned philosophy and the motifs. It must be remembered that every work of Indian architecture — Hindu, Jaina and Buddhist — must first and foremost be regarded from the point of view of its metaphysical aspect, that is, as a kind of replica of some unseen region of which the metaphysical factor determined the plan and elevation. Thus, the temple is the house and body of the deity; its fabric, the very substance of the divinity.

Ritual and dedication contributed to the selection and laying of every piece of material of which the temple was built since this fabric itself was the mystic equivalent of the body of *puruṣa*. The temple is in more ways than one to be thought of as heaven on earth and traditionally ascribed to divine beings. Where Indian architecture is concerned, it is not possible to make any division of styles on any sectarian basis. Hindus, Jainas and Buddhists, all used the same style with slight modifications of structure to meet their ritualistic needs, and as if to lead the worshipper towards the centre of spiritual union with the divine. The sculptural decoration of the temple points the way to that desired union: this is the meaning implicit in the multiple representations in the frieze of *maithunas* or men and women in erotic embrace, which is the ultimate union of the soul with the divine.

It may be noted that as the architects did not take the *maithunas* to mean only human couples but sexual pairs of all kinds of beings, it is reasonable to expect that loving couples would have demanded illustration. But, again, this symbol is not particularly associated with any sectarian cult — Hindu, Jaina or Buddhist. From the very earliest times, it has been appropriated by Buddhist builders as at Sāñcī, Bhārhut, Karlī, Kānherī and Nāsik. Its presence in numerous Hindu temples does not make it peculiarly a Hindu (brāhmana) conception. The temples of Rājpūtānā offer numerous evidences of its use by Jaina builders.

In the art expressions at Ajantā one finds a complete statement of indivisible union of sacred and secular art. In the Ajantā wall-paintings one feels a definite departure from the art of early Buddhism, with its emphasis on the symbolic expressions which were quite apart from the world of reality. There is a sort of religious romanticism, a real lyric quality, a reflexion of the view expressed that every aspect of life has an equal value in the spiritual sense and as an aspect of the divine. Sensuous physical beauty becomes an emblem of spiritual beauty. One is reminded of the Krsna and his scripture, in which he told that all men and women are his form. Here life has become an art, but the ultimate meaning is never forgotten.

The art of India, and its religion and culture absorbed several foreign traits from the central Asian nomadic tribes like the Śakas, the Pārthians and the Kuṣāṇas who reached India. The depiction of the erotic motifs in art was considerably influenced by the socio-cultural milieu of the period. Though secular and sensual interests largely affected its portrayal, some of its earlier aspects were retained. Erotic themes received more romantic touches in their depiction. Sensual and worldly interests are clearly betrayed in the full-bodied and enticing *yakṣīs* or female figures (on the *vedikā*) of Mathurā. An important development during the first-third century AD was the representation of couples and other erotic themes on the door or the entrance of monuments. The motif of *maithuna* in its earliest available portrayal in stone, from the second century BC to the third century AD, underwent major changes including the gradual sensualization of the motif. The profuse use of the *maithuna* motif in art with the increasing sense of depth in sculptures, paved the way for an advancement in the artist's conception of human figures including a development in technique and perception. This suggests that the *maithuna* motif became a socially acceptable form of decoration painting.

The consequent urban development in the early centuries of the era seems to have encouraged taste for voluptuousness in art. Erotic depictions was permitted in religious art because it was considered auspicious. The literature of Bāṇa gives us a picture of life of *nāgarakas* who met occasionally for cultural discussions (*goṣṭhīs*); this kind of gathering gave opportunities for various artistic pursuits. It is this soicial climate that possibly encouraged Vātsyāyana to compile his *Kāmasūtra*. The period also witnessed the plays of Bhāsa and Śūdraka who flourished at the time. From the fifth century AD to the eighth century AD, there was a change in the political scenario which influenced the socio-economic pattern of life. The military powers of the *sāmantas* assumed greater influence and prominence in cultural life and this was also reflected in the arts. The Hindu religion was revived with great fervour. Purāṇic Hinduism was established and charitable works and *dāna* (gift) became an important part of religious life. Another significant development was the rise of Tāntrism. Magical beliefs and practices acquired a great importance under Tāntric cults. From the fifth century onwards we get inscriptional evidences of Tāntric worship. Belief in *Tantra* became a significant factor in influencing the erotic art of the period.

In the Daśāvatāra temple at Deogarh built in about the fifth century AD, *maithunas* were carved on its plinth. This seems to suggest the flexibility in the placement of erotic motifs. In the sixth century AD the depiction of *maithunas* is seen, for the first time, in the temple art of Aihole, Pattadakala, Bādāmī and Mahākūteśvara. Their presence on the door, conventionally associated with auspicious decoration, seems to suggest a magico-religious function of sexual motifs. These sculptures in highly amorous poses indicate that priests and worshippers at this time did not object to the presence of erotic couples on the religious edifices. By this time, the temple was an important socio-religious centre employing the services of different professions. It also provided opportunities for development of arts. The Cave of Bādāmī profusely displays erotic motifs in its art. Sensuous and poetic touches are clearly seen in base-relief over all the pillars and pilasters in the rear wall of the varandah as well as in the *mandapa*, lintels and ceilings, etc. Erotic motifs can also be seen in the Buddhist cave art at Ajantā and Ellorā. The juxtaposition of a nude figure and a *maithuna* scene in an inconspicuous part of the Paraśurāmeśvara temple of Bhuvaneśvara possibly points to its magico-religious function. The other temples having *maithuna* depictions and influenced by Tāntrism are temples of Bhuvaneśvara, Kailāsanātha Cave of Ellorā, Someśvara temple of Mukhaliṅgam. But the depiction of *maithuna* was not acceptable at all. The period reveals a contrast in the treatment of *mithuna* and *maithuna* themes: the former was accepted as a convention, and the latter had to make its way into the *śilpa* rules. It is an interim period and represents *maithuna* before it was conventionalized in temple art. We should note here that some of the shrines associated with Tāntrism do not have any depiction of *maithuna* in their art.

The temple architecture from eighth to ninth century onwards provided opportunities for the exhibition of artistic talents and the power of wealth. Temple building was one of the means of satisfying the patrons. It gave emotional expression to their needs of fame and glory as well as *puṇya* (merit). There was a competitive spirit among the royal families for building large and magnificent temples. Every king wanted to surpass his ancestor or his neighbour in building temples. The art of the temple, which is a sacred place, became an exhibition of the charity of the donor and the skill of the artist. The temple house and the body of god became a piece of art. This is the only period in Indian history when temples were built on a mass scale. Superstition and belief in magic held sway over the people at the same time and regional outlooks influenced the cultural pursuits. The temples, Hindu and Buddhist, were not only a place of religious worship but also a centre of socio-cultural activities. The *Pāśupata* and *Kālāmukha* sects acquired the position of chief priests in many medieval temples, especially of Gujarat, Mysore and Kaśmīr. The atmosphere of the medieval temple was a breeding ground for luxurious living and degenerated sexual practices. The institution of *devadāsī* also vitiated the atmosphere of the temple. The *Purānas* advocated offerings of girls to the temple. The services of *devadāsīs* became popular in the religious life of the medieval period. Special architectural arrangements were made in both the Hindu and Jaina medieval temples for performance of dance, drama and music — activities associated with the temples since the ancient times. We find references of such activities in the writings of Patañjali, Bāna, Kālidāsa, Bhavabhūti, Dandin and many others. The medieval temple is to be viewed against this aristocratic and affluent background, far from the ideals of Upanisadic asceticism.

From the third century BC to the seventh century AD, Indian art had a common denominator; but from the eighth century onwards the regional spirit in art gradually asserted itself. Curiously enough, in spite of the passage of time, the classical tradition of Indian art is still being maintained in places. In the treatment of erotic motifs, we clearly see regional variations. The attitude towards erotic depiction seems to be different in each region. The place allotted to the erotic motifs on the temples is in accordance with the architectural canons of the region. But the sectarian affiliation of the temples is not the determining factor in the treatment of erotic motifs on the temples. The sexual representation is seen on Hindu temples of all sects — even the rare shrine of Brahmā in Gujarāt has the representation of coital couples. Jaina and Buddhist shrines of the medieval period are also not free from erotic display. It can thus be concluded that, in general, the nature of sexual representation was not determined to any significant extent either in theme or in form by the kind of religious sect to which the temple belonged. For instance, there is nothing *Śaiva* of *Śākta* or *Vaisnava* in the treatment accorded to the erotic motifs on the temples. The Pārśvanāth temple of Khajurāho and Ratnāgiri in Orissa are among a few Tāntric Jain and Buddhist shrines depicting sexual scenes. It was an auspicious motif accepted in the art of the period. Their presence seems to fulfil some particular function: they probably suggest the prevalance of some strong belief, not necessarily connected with any religious sect, which may have been associated with a religious substratum common to the religions.

There is an explanation for the sexual motifs based primarily on the philosophical concepts of the *Upaniṣads*, according to which, the function of erotic motifs on the temples would be to convey the non-dual state of the Highest Reality. But this explanation is inadequate; it fails to account for the existence of numerous sculptures depicting gross sexuality. Another view may be that erotic figures are an expression of *kāma*, the third *puruṣārtha* (*dharma*, *artha*, *kāma* and *mokṣa* being the four *puruṣārthas*). But *kāma* is only subservient to *dharma*; it is not an end itself. Unrestrained gratification of sexual urges was never prescribed in religious texts.

Many religious and philosophical movements contributed their different hues to the multi-coloured canvas of the ancient culture of India. The ultimate aim of life is to attain release (*mokṣa*) and art is one means of attaining this aim. So much ado has been made about the frank eroticism of the sculptures of the religious shrines that, perhaps, now is the time for a valid observation. A creative sensuousness has always been regarded as an important source of energy, of a vital urge in life, as much in religious and spiritual quest as in the quest for expression; and the *maithuna* idea of this *sādhanā* finds a most creative expression. Indeed it was accepted as a normal and essential part of life without any shame or secrecy attached to it as indicated by the temples of Purī and Konārka, where admittedly the eroticism is not only in the sensuous suggestiveness but in the depiction of sexual acts in a wide variety of poses and attitudes as well.

The pivot of early medieval sculpture was the human figure in the form of gods and goddesses. The cult image was mainly conceived as an object to be used by the devotee to help him in focusing his mind for the realisation of an ultimate object outside the image itself. This image had no inherent relation either with the devotee or with the artist; it existed apart from him and was identical neither with his inner experience nor with his ultimate object.

The depiction of couples on terracotta are representative of ritualistic pairs in fertility rites. The portrayal of couples on stone monuments indicate an auspicious function. In the early medieval period, the depiction of erotic pairs seems to have been magico-religious in function. After the ninth century AD, the acceptance of sexual motifs in one form or the other by all the religious groups suggests the prevalance of some beliefs in connection with the depiction of sex. However, the portrayal of ascetics in sexual acts seems to be far from the goal of the yogic ideal of *mokṣa* (for attaining *sahaja* state). These scenes may be *Tāntrika*, but public display of the practices contradicts the basic tenets of Tāntrism which was highly secretive in nature. *Tāntrika* orgies of *cakrapūjā* would very probably correspond where many pairs participate in a simultaneous orgy. The basic under-currents behind sexual depiction has to be magico-religious beliefs and practice associated with sex, as found in fertility rites in general and Tāntrism in particular. Erotic sculptures are influenced not by any philosophical symbolism but by those religious beliefs and practices which reflect the primal connection between sex and religion.

In the medieval period religious cults were influenced by Tāntrism and every god was given a female partner known as Śakti or *prajñā*. *Tāntrika* literature and beliefs gave impetus to the worship of gods with their consorts which is also reflected in medieval iconography. Temples of Bhuvaneśvara, Khajurāho, Kadwana, Nāgdā, Bagalī, Belūr, Halebid, Somanāthpura, Ambernāth have representations of deities in pairs and in amorous attitudes along with their *śakti*s. Female and male genitals, known as *yoni* and *liṅgam* in India, are worshipped and considered to be endowed with power and grace. In India, the Pāśupatas enshrined *liṅga*s to commemorate the dead teacher. The *Nāthpanthī*s, who buried their dead instead of following the Hindu practice of cremation, represented the symbol of *yoni-liṅga* on their graves. The body of the *yogī* who has attained liberation is identified with Śiva and hence, the symbol of the latter is represented on the grave. The *Pāśupatas*, the *Kālāmukhas* and the *Śaiva-Siddhāntins* were given the highest position in the temple-organization in many places of India.

Tāntrism was a powerful religious movement which emerged out of the coalescence between primitive magic and highly evolved spiritual ideals. Tāntric practices are older than the written scripture on the subject. Their systematic introduction into Hinduism, Jainism and Buddhism took place in about the fifth century AD. The period of seventh to twelfth centuries were the peak periods of the Tāntric cults of the Hindus, Jainas and Buddhists. Buddhist Tāntrism was prevalent in Orissā, Bengāl and Bihār. The Hindu shrines of Bhuvaneśvara show the amalgamation of *Pāśupata*, *Śākta* and Buddhist Tāntric influences in their iconography. Images of the time of the Pāla dynasty show Tāntric influences.[6] The monasteries of Nālandā, Pahārpura and Ratnāgari were centres of Buddhist Tāntrism. The cult of *yoginīs* was prevalent at Khajurāho and Bheraghāṭ in about the ninth and tenth centuries AD.

Do the erotic figures on temples represent Tāntric *sādhakas* in the non-dual state of divine bliss? We know that this *sādhanā* was not meant for pleasure but was undertaken as a ritual and in this light, a very few sculptures were found relieved according to *Haṭha*-yogic discipline. Moreover, the male figures are often shown with protruding stomachs or disproportionate bodies which indicate that they were not adept in *Haṭha-yoga*. The eternal bliss of the non-dual state is rarely reflected in the sculptural depictions. Only some sculptures of Orissā and Khajurāho present lovers in a state of bliss. The esoteric rites (*vidhis*) of Pāśupata, who influenced many *aghorī tāntrika* sects, are considered relevant in explaining some of the erotic depictions on the temples by the famous iconographists. But it is a contradiction that the *tāntrika* esoteric doctrines were exposed to the general public. The initiated persons were not to expose their practices in front of the common people. Only specially initiated persons (*vīra* type not *paśus*) had the privilege of practising the ritual of sex. *Tāntrika* literature advocates strict secrecy of the rituals. The true *tāntrika* art is functionally related to *upāsanā* and *sādhanā* to attain the non-dual *sahaja* state. The theory of the *maṇḍala* or mystic circle, *yantras* or mystic diagrams aided the *sādhaka* to reach his spiritual goal. Such art is not decorative as it is cultic. The *tāntrika* shrines of India are not associated with erotic display.

Some temples have erotic figures, but do they show the influence of the regional style of art in their portrayal? The depiction of erotic motifs is within the sphere of art, which has had a long tradition since the remote past. Conventions and the relationship of Tāntrism to sexual depiction has to be viewed in the historical perspective. The *mithuna* (amorous couple) has been traditionally accepted in Indian art as an auspicious symbol since the historical period. In the sixth century, the *maithuna* scenes are seen on the door of Aihole temples in place of non-coital *mithuna* of early art.

Tāntrism was the major factor in bringing about the transformation in depiction from *mithuna* to *maithuna*. The change in the depiction was due to social permissiveness and the influence of Tāntrism. Ritualistic sex gradually acquired a hedonistic tinge. The Tāntric concept of *maithuna* as *makāra* rested on the use of sex for achieving *siddhis* and as a means for easily gaining *moksa*; instead of the rigorous path of asceticism, Tāntrism was one way to achieve this. The sexual representations in religious art lies in the idea of fertility rites seen the worldover. The central idea is that religious and secular aspects of sex were operative behind erotic depiction in temples and the interest in sex as *bhoga*, which was cultivated for its own sake rather than for religious purposes. This is also found in literary works including poems dealing with religious themes which were endowed with sensuality and a worldly consciousness that is seen in temple sculptures where there is nothing spiritual in expression or association. However, the attributes of prosperity, fruitfulness and fertility are still associated with erotic motifs. The cultic function was associated and superseded by the aesthetic and the sensual.

The erotic temple sculpture is not *tāntrika* art, but art as influenced by Tāntrism without being functionally related to *tāntrika sādhanā*.

## References

1. *Svetāśvara Upaniṣad*, VI.23.
2. J. Marshall, *Mohenjo-daro and the Indus Civilization*, London, 1930, pp. 52-55 and 59.
3. *Indian Archaeology — A Review*, 1958-59, fig. 7.
4. D.H. Gordon, *Pre-historic Background of Indian Culture*, Bombay, 1958, p. 116.
5. *IAR*, 1962-63, pp. 5-6; Motichand, *Lalitkala*, No. 8, pp. 8-9.
6. Buddhism of the Pāla and Sena Period represents that outgrowth of *Mahāyāna* which is described as Tāntrism, an assimilation of elements of Hindu religion into Buddhism, such as concepts of Śakti or female energy of the *bodhisattva*, and reliance on magic spells and rituals. The worship of the mystical *Dhyānī* Buddhas and the Creator. Ādi-Buddhas, a Buddhist Brahmā, completely replace any devotion to the person of the mortal Buddha. This phase of Buddhism is described as the *Vajrayāna*, that together with the paraphernalia of its art, in the eighth and ninth centuries, took on the principal aspects of Tāntric Śaivism and Vaiṣṇavism.

# Visuals

*Ill.* 1. *Mṛtyuñjaya-Śiva* (Conqueror of Death).

Ill. 2. *Hiraṇyagarbha* (Cosmic Egg).

*Ill.* 3. *Śiva-Śakti* — Śiva manifests Himself before Kṛṣṇa and chief priest.

Ill. 4. *Chinnamastā*.

Ill. 5. Śiva-Liṅga.

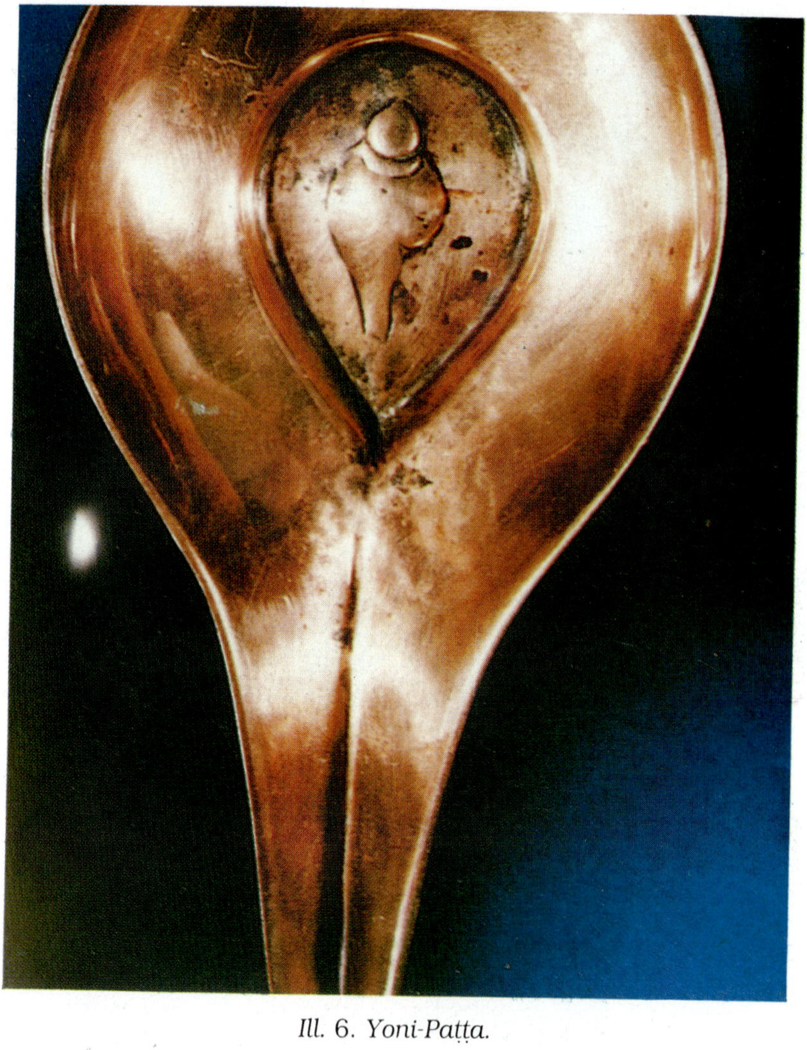

*Ill. 6. Yoni-Paṭṭa.*

Ill. 7. *Prajñapāramitā.*

*Ill. 8. A Devotee with Śiva-Liṅga.*

Pl. 9. Oṁ.

*Ill.* 10. *Erotic Sculpture.*

*Ill.* 11. *Kalyāṇa Sunder* (Marriage of Śiva and Pārvatī).

*Ill. 12. Bhairava.*

नग्यान सुभाऊ ॥ जो देपा सोसनानस्काऊ ॥ देषी माया स ।
बविधिगाही ॥ अतिसभीतजो रेक रहाही ॥ देषाजीवन चावै ।
जादी ॥ देषी भक्ति जुज्ञरैताही ॥ तनपुलकितमुषवचन ।
श्रावा ॥ नयनसदिचरनि सिरनावा ॥

*Ill. 13. Viśvarūpa Viṣṇu* — Rāma's mystical appearance before Kauśalyā.

*Ill.* 14. *Hanu-Bhairava.*

*Ill.* 15. *Dancing Gaṇeśa.*

Ill. 16. *Celestial Woman with Flowers.*

*Ill. 17. Cakra-Puruṣa.*

*Ill. 18. Hairuka.*

*Ill. 19..Mañjuśrī.*

*Ill. 20. Cakra, Maṇḍala and Trikoṇa.*

*Ill.* 21A. *Cakra* (*Wheel*).

*Ill.* 21B. *Cakra* (*Wheel*).

*Ill. 22. Śiva-Temple.*

*Ill. 23. Kandariya Mahādeva.*

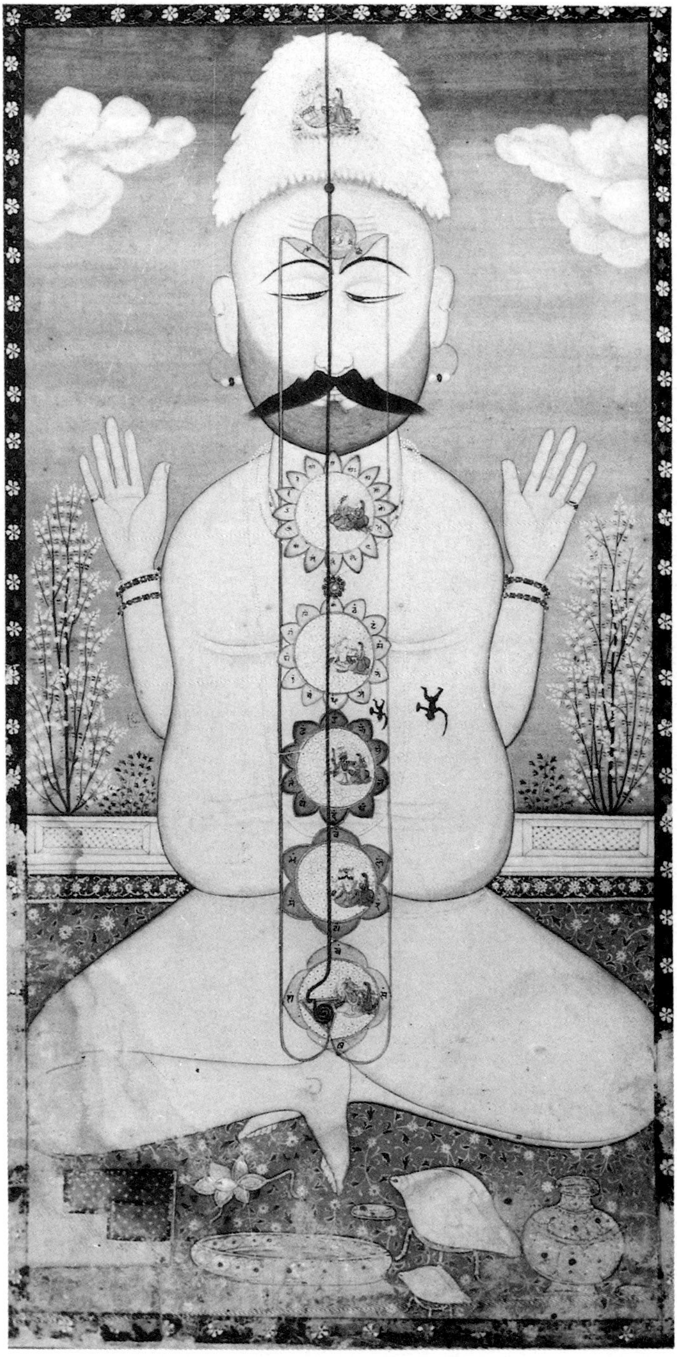

Ill. 24. *Sat-dal-Kamala.*

*Ill. 25. Buddha.*

Ill. 26. *Alasa Kanyā.*

*Ill. 27: Linga-Yoni*

*Ill. 28. Sun.*

# Bibliography

Abhinavaguptacharya : *Sri Tantra Loka*, Part IV, Srinagar (Govt. Publication), 1922.

Acharya, Narendra Deo : *Bauddha Dharma Darśana*, Patna, 1956.

Agrawal, Vasudeo Saran : *Harṣa Carita : Eak Sānskritic Adhyayana*, (in Hindi), Patna, 1964.

——— : *Śiva-Mahādeo*, Patna, 1966.

Allchin, Bridget and Raymond : *The Birth of Indian Civilization*, Great Britain, 1968.

Anand, Mulk Raj and Lance Dane : *Kāma Sūtra of Vātsyāyana*, New Delhi, 1982.

——— : *Kāma-Kalā*, New York, 1958.

Apte, Vamana Shivarama : *Sanskrit Hindi Kośa*, Varanasi, 1966.

Bagachi, P.C. : *Studies in the Tantras*, Part I, Calcutta, 1939.

——— : *Pre-Dravidian and Pre-Aryan in India*, Calcutta, 1929.

——— : *Kaulajñāna nirnaya and Some Minor Texts of the School of Matsyendranāth*, Calcutta, 1934.

Banerjea, J.N. : *The Development of Hindu Iconography*, Calcutta, 1956.

——— : *Paurāṇic and Tāntric Religion*. Calcutta, 1966.

Basham, A.L. : *A Cultural History of India*, London, 1975.

Basu, Manoranjan : *Tantras, A General Study*, Calcutta, 1976.

Bhandarkar, R.G. : *Vaiṣṇavism, Śaivism and Minor Religious Systems*, (reprint), Varanasi, 1965.

Bharati, Agehananda : *Tāntric Tradition*, New Delhi, 1983.

Bhattacharya, B.T. : *An Introduction to the Buddhist Esotericism*, London, 1932.

——— : *Indian Buddhist Iconography*, Calcutta, 1959.

Bhattacharya, N.N. : *The Indian Mother Goddess*, New Delhi, 1977.

——— : *The History of Śākta Religion* Delhi, 1974.

——— : *Ancient Indian Rituals*, New Delhi, 1975.

——— : *The History of the Tāntric Religion*, New Delhi, 1982.

——— : *The History of Indian Erotic Literature*, New Delhi, 1975.

Bhattacharya, Tarapada : *The Canons of Indian Art*, Calcutta, 1963.

Bose, D.N. and Haldhar, Hira Lal : *Tantra : Their Philosophy and Occult Secrets*, Calcutta, 1981.

Bramha, Nalani Kant : *Philosophy of Hindu Sādhanā*, London, 1932.

Briggs, G.W. : *Gorakha Nāth and the Kanphaṭa Yogis*, Calcutta, 1938.

Chakravarti, C. : *Tantras, Studies on their Religion and Literature*, Calcutta, 1963.

Chaturvedi, Sitaram : *Kālidāsa Granthāvalī*, (Sanskrit-Hindi), Varanasi, 1980.

——— : *Cultural Heritage of India*, Vol. I-IX, ed. by H. Bhattacharya, Ram Krishna Institute, Calcutta.

Dasgupta, S.N. : *An Introduction to Tāntric Buddhism*, Calcutta, 1974.

——— : *Aspects of Indian Religious Thought*, Calcutta, 1957.

——— : *Obscure Religious Cults*, 2nd edn., Calcutta, 1962.

Datta, R.C. : *Prācin Bhārat Kī Sabhyatā Kā Itihāsa* (in Hindi), Allahabad, 1966.

De, Sushil Kumar : *Ancient Indian Erotics and Erotics-Literature*, Calcutta, 1959.

Desai, Devangana : *Erotic Sculpture of India* : A Socio-Cultural Study, Delhi, 1975.

Deussen, Paul : *The Philosophy of the Upaniṣad*, (reprint), New Delhi, 1979.

Dwivedi, Hazari Prasad : *Nāth Sampradāya* (in Hindi), Allahabad, 1959.

Eggeling, J. tr. : *Śatapatha Brāhmaṇa*, 1963.

Gardon, D.H. : *Pre-Historic Background of Indian Culture*, Bombay, 1958.

Gunther, H.V. : *Yuganaddha, the Tāntric View of Life*, (2nd edn.), Banaras, 1964.

Gupta, Sanjukta : *Prapañcasāra*, Leiden, 1972.

——— : *Hayvajra Tantra*, ed. and tr. by D.L. Snellgrove, London, 1959.

——— : History and Culture of Indian People, ed. by R.C.

Majumdar, A.D. Pusalker & A.K. Majumdar, Vol. I to X, Bombay.

——: *The Age of Imperial Kanauj*, Vol. IV.

——: *Indian Archaeology — A Review*, 1958-59, and 1962-63.

——: *Indian Historical Quarterly*, March, 1933.

John Woodroffe : *Principles of Tantras*, Madras, 1952.

Joshi, Lalmani : *Studies in Buddhist Culture of India*, Banaras, 1967.

Joshi, Pandit Harishankar : *Vedic Viswadarshan*, Banaras Hindu University, Varanasi, 1966.

——: *Kalyāṇa*, (Śivāṅka), Saṁvat, 1990, Gita Press, Gorakhpur.

——: *Klyāṇa* (Śāktyāṅk), Saṁvat, 1991, Gita Press, Gorakhpur.

Kane, P.V. : *History of Dharmaśāstra*, 5 vols., Poona, 1962.

Kaviraj, Gopinath : *Journal of Ganga Nath Jha Research Institute*, Vol. III, Allahabad.

——: *Tāntric Sāhitya*, (in Hindi), Lucknow, 1972.

——: *Gopinath Kaviraj Abhinandan Grantha*, Lucknow, 1967.

——: *Bhāratīya Sanskṛti Aur Sādhanā*, (in Hindi), Part I & II, Patna, 1963 & 1964.

——: *Tantra-Sangraha*, Varanasi, 1970.

——: *Tāntric Vāṅgamaya Aur Śākta Dṛṣṭi*, (in Hindi), Patna, 1963.

Keith, A.B. : *The Religion and Philosophy of Veda and Upanishad*, Varanasi, 1965.

——— : *Taittirīya Saṁhitā*, Varanasi, 1967.

———: *Ṛgveda Brāhmaṇas, Aitareya and Kauśītaki Brāhmaṇas of the Ṛgveda*, 1920.

——— : *The Karma Mīmāṁsā*, London, 1921.

Kosambi, D.D. : *Myth and Reality*, Bombay, 1962.

Lorenzen, D.N. : *The Kāpālikas and Kālāmukhas*, (Two Lost Śaivite Sects), New Delhi, 1972.

Marshall, J. : *Mohenjodaro and Indus Civilization*, London, 1930.

Max Müllar : *The Upaniṣad*, Delhi, 1965.

Mishra, T.N. : *Bhāratīya Prācya Sāhitya mein Śiva Kā Svarūpa*, Parisad Patrikā, Verṣa 25, Aṅk 3, 1985, Patna.

Mookerjee, Ajit : *Tantra Āsana*, New Delhi, 1971.

——— : *Tantra Art*, New Delhi, 1971.

——— : *The Tāntric Way*, London, 1977.

——— : *Navonmeṣa*, M.M. Gopinath Kaviraj Smṛti Granth (in Hindi), Varanasi, 1987.

Pant, Ramesha Chandra : *Early Hindu Civilization*, Calcutta, 1963.

Pathak, V.S. : *The History of Saiva Cults in Northern India*, Varanasi, 1960.

Pusalker, A.D. : *Studies in the Epics and Purāṇas*, Bombay, 1955.

Radhakrishnan, S. : *Principal Upaniṣads*, London, 1953.

——— : *The Hindu View of Life*, London, 1957.

——— : *The Brahma Sūtra*, The Philosophy of Spiritual Life,

London, 1960.

——— : *History of Philosophy, Eastern and Western*, London, 1952.

Rao, T.A. Gopi Nath : *Elements of Hindu Iconography*, Vol. I & II, Madras.

Rockhill, W.W. : *The Life of Buddha*, (reprint), Varanasi, 1972.

Rhys-Davids, T.W. : *Buddhism*, London, 1920.

Sastri, Gopal : *Manusmriti*, Varanasi, 1982.

——— : *Manusmriti or Law of Manu*, tr. by G. Buhler, *S.B.E.*, Vol. XXV, 1964.

Sastri, Hara Prasad : *Advaya Sangraha*, Gayakwada Oriental Series, Baroda, 1927.

Sastri, Manamatha Nath : *Agni Purāṇa*, Varanasi, 1967.

Shastri, Mahadeva : *Brahman Sutra (Śāṅkara Bhāṣya)*, 1915.

Satavalakar, Sripada Damodar : *Mahābhārata*, Parodi.

Sharma, L.N. : *Kāśmīr Śaivism*, Varanasi, 1972.

Sharma, Neela Kamal : *Prācīn Bharata Mein Śakti Pūjā* (in Hindi), Poona, 1986.

Sharma, R.S. : *Aspects of Political Ideas and Institutions in Ancient India*, New Delhi, 1959.

——— : *Indian Feudalism* : 300-1200, Calcutta, 1965.

Sharma, Shiva Dutta : *Nirukta*, 1904.

Shukla, Vanshidhar : *Vāmamārga* (in Hindi), Allahabad, 1951.

Singh, Amar : *Amara Kośa*, Chowkhamba Sanskrit Series, Varanasi, 1970.

Singh, Bhagawati Prasad : *Maṇīsī Kī Lokayātrā* (in Hindi),

Varanasi, 1980.

Singh, Ram Dular (ed.) : *Aghora Granthāvalī*, (in Hindi), 1986.

Sinha, B.C. : *Hinduism and Symbol Worship*, Delhi, 1983.

Srinivasachari, P.N. : *Advaita and Visiṣṭādvaita*, Bombay, 1961.

Tatia, N. : *Studies in Jaina Philosophy*, Banaras, 1951.

Tripathi, L.K., Erotic Scenes of Khajurāho, Bulletin of the College of Indology, Banaras Hindu University, No. 3, 1959-60, Varanasi.

Upadhyaya, Baldev : *Bhāratīya Darśana* (in Hindi), Varanasi, 1966.

Upadhyay, Nagendra Nath : *Bauddha Kāpālika Sādhanā Aur Sāhitya*, (in Hindi), Allahabad, 1983.

——— : *Tāntric Bauddha Sādhana Aur Sāhitya*, (in Hindi), Kashi Saṁvat, 2015.

Wayman, Alex : "Female Energy and Symbolism in the Buddhist Tantra", *History of Religion*, Vol. II, No. 1, 1962.

William, M. : *A Sanskrit to English Dictionary*. London, 1956.

Williams, R. : *Jaina Yoga*, London, 1963.

Winternitz, M. : *History of Sanskrit Literature*, 3 Vols., Delhi, 1972.

Woodroffe, J. : *The Serpent Power, being the Satcakra-Nirupan*, Madras, 1958.

——— : "Great Liberation", (*Mahānirvāṇa Tantra*), Madras, 1953.

Zimmer, H. : *The Art of Indian Asia*, New York, 1955.

——— : *Myth and Symbols in Indian Art and Civilization*,

U.S.A., 1963.

## Classical Works

——— : *Atharvaveda* (in Hindi) by Satavalakar, Parodi, 1989.

——— : *Bhagavad Gītā*, Gorakhpur, Saṁvat 2040.

——— : *Bṛhadāraṇyaka Upaniṣad*, Varanasi, 1983.

——— : *Chāndogya Upaniṣad*, Gita Press, Gorakhpur, Saṁvat 2013.

——— : *Devī Bhāgavata*, Sastri, Ram Tej, Varanasi, 1965.

——— : *Haṭhayogapradīpikā*, tr. by Pancham Singh, Allahabad, 1955.

——— : *Jaiminīya Brāhmaṇa*.

——— : *Jānārṇava Tantra*, ed. by G.S. Gokhale, Poona, 1952.

——— : *Kaṭhopaniṣad*, Varanasi, 1983.

——— : *Kauśītaki Brāhmaṇa*.

——— : *Kena Upaniṣad*, Varanasi, 1983.

——— : *Kulārṇava Tantra*, Tāntrik text, Vol. V, London, 1917.

——— : *Māṇḍukyopaniṣad*, Gita Press, Gorakhpur.

——— : *Mantra Mahodadhi*.

——— : *Muṇḍaka Upaniṣad*, ed. by Vidya Nand Giri, Rishikesh, 1978.

——— : *Paraśurām Kalp Sūtra*, (Gaekwad's Oriental Series, Vols. XXII-XXIII).

——— : *Ṛgveda*, (in Hindi), ed. by Satavalakara, Parodi, 1983.

——— : *Rudra Yāmala*, Calcutta, 1937.

——— : *Sakti Sangam*, (G.O.S. Nos. LXI, XCI, CIV), Baroda, 1932-47.

——— : *Śāradātilak*, Tantrik texts, Vols. XVI, XVII, Calcutta, 1933.

——— : *Saundarya Laharī*, ed. by A. Kuppuswami, New Delhi, 1991.

——— : *Sivamahimna Strotram*, (reprint), Varanasi, 1964.

——— : *Śrī Tattva Cintāmaṇi*.

——— : *Svetāśvatara Upaniṣad*, tr. by Ram Swarupa Sharma, Bombay, 1913.

——— : *Taittirīya Upaniṣad*, Gita Press, Gorakhpur.

——— : *Sacred Book of the East : The Vedānta Sūtras*, Vol. 34 and 38 (in 2 Vols.) with Śaṅkarācārya Commentary. Sacred Books of the East : *The Vedānta-Sūtras*, with Rāmānuja Śrī Bhāṣya, Vol. XLVIII, Delhi.

——— : *Sacred Book of the Hindus*, ed. by Basu, B.D.

——— : *Standard English-Hindi Dictionary*, 2nd edn., Allahabad, 1983.

# Glossary

*Ācāra* : Rule.

*Ādinātha* : Primal lord.

*Advaya/Advaita* : Non-dualism.

*Ādyā-Śakti* : Primordial energy conceived as a goddess.

*Aghora* : One of the five forms of Śiva.

Agni : Fire.

*Aikya* : Unity.

*Ajapā* : A special form of meditation.

*Ājñācakra* : One of the six nerve-plexuses situated between the eyebrows.

*Ākāśa* : Space.

*Akula* : The Śiva aspect of Śakti. According to Abhinavagupta, that which is manifested from *Kula* or *Śakti* is *Akula* and it is endowed with the elements of Śiva.

*Amṛta* : Nectar.

*Anādi* : That which has no beginning.

*Anāhata* : One of the six nerve-plexuses (*ṣaṭcakra*) situated in the heart region. *Anāhata* is also the name of a particular form of sound.

*Ānanda* : Bliss.

*Ānandamaya-kośa* : Sheath of bliss.

| | |
|---|---|
| *Ānnamaya-kośa* | : Sheath of bliss. |
| *Aṅśa* | : Part. |
| *Antarātmā* | : Inner soul. |
| *Aṇu* | : The term, atom. |
| *Anugraha* | : Grace. |
| *Aparā* | : The term for material or lower knowledge. |
| *Ardhanārīśvara* | : The half-woman and half-man. |
| *Artha* | : One of the four *puruṣārthas* denoting wealth or material prosperity. The term is also used to denote 'meaning' and expression. |
| *Āsana* | : Posture. |
| *Aṣṭakoṇa-cakra* | : Octagonal diagram said to be the extension of *trikoṇa-cakra* or triangular diagram. |
| *Ātmadarśana* | : Self-realisation. |
| *Ātmaśakti* | : Power of the self. |
| *Avadhūta* | : The aspirant who commands universal reverence. |
| *Avidyā* | : Ignorance. |
| *Avyakta* | : The unmanifested. A synonym of *Prakṛti* or primordial substance. |
| *Āyurveda* | : Indian indigenous system of medicine. |
| *Bhakti* | : Devotion. |
| *Bhāṇḍa* | : Body. |
| *Bhāva* | : Disposition; state; mental certitude. |
| *Bhīmā* | : The frightful. |
| *Bhoga* | : Enjoyment. |
| *Bhūta* | : Śiva; living being; the world; one of the five elements. |

| | |
|---|---|
| *Bīja* | Seed; in *tantra* it signifies the germ-syllable which takes the form of a deity. It is also the term for semen. |
| *Bodhi* | Knowledge. |
| *Bodhicitta* | Enlightenment. |
| *Brahmāṇḍa* | Cosmic egg. |
| *Buddhi* | Intelligence. |
| *Caitanya* | Consciousness; in internal worship the aspirant has to think that the goddess is enshrined within his body as pure-consciousness or the self. |
| *Cakra* | Circle; used in a variety of senses, symbolising endless rotation of *śakti*. |
| Cāmuṇḍā/Caṇḍī/Caṇḍikā | The wrathful. |
| *Candra* | Moon. |
| *Caryā* | Observance. |
| *Cit* | Intelligence or consciousness. |
| *Cit-śakti* | The principle of consciousness. |
| *Cittabhūmi* | The plane of mind. |
| *Cittaśuddhi* | Purification of mind. |
| *Dakṣina-mārga* | It is the path of spiritual attainment without the use of *pañca-makāra* and other extreme forms of rituals. |
| *Dāna* | Gift. |
| *Deha* | Body. |
| *Dharma* | Religion. |
| *Dharma-kāya* | Word of Buddha. |
| *Dhvani* | Sound. |
| *Digambara/ Digambarī* | Space clad; naked. |

| | | |
|---|---|---|
| *Dīkṣā* | : | Initiation as an essential condition of Tāntric *sādhanā*. |
| *Divya* | : | Divine; Superior. |
| *Dyau* | : | Heaven. |
| *Dyāvāpṛthivī* | : | Heaven and Earth. |
| *Grāhya* | : | Perceivable. |
| *Grāhyaka* | : | Perceiver. |
| *Guhya* | : | Secret. |
| *Guṇa* | : | Quality. |
| *Guru* | : | The preceptor or teacher who is the pivot in Tāntric *sādhanā*. *Guru* is one who dispels darkness. |
| *Haṁsa* | : | A symbolic *mantra* in the form of breath. *Haṃ* is the symbol of *vindu* (*puruṣa* — male principle of creation) and *saḥ* of *visarga* (*prakṛti* — the female principle of creation). |
| *Haṭhayoga* | : | A form of physical exercise for making the body so disciplined as to serve all spiritual purposes. In *Haṭhayoga Pradīpikā*, 1.10 it is regarded as the source of all forms of *yoga*. |
| *Icchā* | : | Will. |
| *Icchā-Śakti* | : | Volition. |
| *Iḍā* | : | One of the four principal nerves. As the symbol of moon, it is situated on the left side of the spinal cord. |
| *Iśāna* | : | One of the Rudras. |
| *Īṣṭa* | : | Desired. |
| *Jīva* | : | Soul. |

| | | |
|---|---|---|
| *Jivanmukti* | : | Liberation with span of bodily existence, a very important Tāntric concept. He who has complete grasp of the knowledge of the self, has dispelled from within the darkness of false knowledge by constant practice and meditation and is reaping the fruits of his *karma*, may be called a *jivanmukti*. |
| *Jīvātmā* | : | Individual soul. |
| *Jñāna* | : | Knowledge; Philosophical knowledge. |
| *Jñāna-śakti* | : | Cognition. |
| *Kaivalya* | : | Isolation, detachment of soul from matter or further transmigration. |
| *Kalā* | : | Evolutes of *varṇa*. It denotes *prakṛti*, *śakti* and *māyā* and Absolute transcendental power. |
| *Kāla* | : | Time. |
| *Kāla-cakra* | : | *Kāla-cakra* denoting wheel of time is the principal god of the Tāntric Buddhist *Kāla Cakrayāna*. |
| *Kāma* | : | Desire; Passion. |
| *Kāma-bīja* | : | Vital fluid. |
| *Kāma-vāyu* | : | Wind passion. |
| *Kāraṇa* | : | Tāntric term for wine. |
| *Karma* | : | Action. |
| *Karuṇā* | : | Compassion. |
| *Kaula* | : | Non-duality. |
| *Kavaca* | : | Amulets; armour, which saves the body from weapons. |
| *Kāyā* | : | Body. |
| *Kriyā* | : | Action or activities. |

| | | |
|---|---|---|
| *Kriyā-śakti* | : | Administration. |
| *Kula* | : | Clan or family. |
| *Kulapatha* | : | The way through which *kuṇḍalinī* pierces the *ṣaṭcakra*. Way of *kaula*. |
| *Kuṇḍalinī* | : | The serpent power remaining latent in the *mūlādhāra*. |
| *Latā* | : | The female partner of the aspirant. |
| *Latā sādhanā* | : | *Pañca-makāra* rituals with the female partner. |
| *Laya yoga* | : | The higher form of *Haṭhayoga* which destroys (*laya*) all forms of desire. It is an experience of eternal bliss in which the mind totally merges in the supreme being. |
| *Līlā* | : | Divine play. |
| *Liṅga* | : | Male generative organ worshipped as a phallic symbol. *Liṅga* is the symbol of Śiva. |
| *Liṅgāṅga* | : | *Liṅga* = Śiva + *Aṅga* = Soul (*ātmā*). |
| *Madhyamā* | : | Name of a special type of sound which is between *paśyanti* and *vaikhari*. It is also called a state of equilibrium of *parā* and *paśyanti*. |
| *Madya* | : | The first of the five *makāras*. Any type of wine, purified by *mantra*, is fit for *sādhanā*. |
| *Mahā* | : | Great; Supreme. |
| *Mahāsukha* | : | Blissful condition; great bliss. |
| Maheśvara | : | Great Lord. |
| *Maithuna* | : | Sexual intercourse which is regarded as one of the five *makāras*. For spiritual |

| | | |
|---|---|---|
| | | interpretation **see** *Kulārṇva*, V; Non-duality. |
| *Māṃsa* | : | Flesh — one of the five *makāras*. It is supposed to be body of Śiva. |
| *Maṇḍala* | : | A special gathering of aspirants for collective rituals of the five *makāras* where they sit in a circle (*cakra*) with their female partners; Mystic circle. |
| *Maṇipūra* | : | A nerve (*cakra*) plexus near the naval region. It is also called *nābhicakra*. |
| *Manomaya-kośa* | : | Sheath of lower mind. |
| *Mantra* | : | Power (*śakti*) in the form of sound; words and letters. It (*mantra*) is ultimate reality in the form of sound. |
| *Mātṛkā* | : | Divine Mothers. It is also the name of mystic letters. |
| *Matsya* | : | Fish — which is one of the five *makāras*; symbolically, *matsya* is described as that which destroys the fetters and leads to the path of salvation. |
| *Māyā* | : | Illusion, false knowledge, material cause of creation, etc. |
| *Māyin* | : | Maheśvara. |
| *Mithuna* | : | Amorous couple. |
| *Moharātri* | : | Night of bewilderment. |
| *Mokṣa* | : | Salvation (*nirvāṇa*). |
| *Mudra* | : | *Mudrā* is also the name of one of the five *makāras*. In Buddhist *tantra*, *mudrā* is used exclusively for the woman and her generative organ; gesture. |
| *Mukti* | : | Salvation (*nirvāṇa*). |

*Mūlādhāra* : The first of the six nerve plexuses, it is situated in the lowest extremity of the spinal cord where the *kuṇḍalanī* is coiled.

*Nāda* : (a) Sound. (b) A term used in *Tantra* in a variety of senses. Its simple meaning is sound. In Tāntric concepts, the supreme being (*parā-śiva* or *parā-śakti*) is soundless and without any vibration. When this *parā-śakti* goes to express itself in creation its first vibration is known as *nāda*. It is the manifestation of the consciousness of the supreme being revealed as sound. This manifestation is thought of in terms of the copulation of Śiva and Śakti (the static and kinetic aspects, also known as *prakāśa* and *vimarśa*, of the same ultimate reality) and the thrill of the pleasure of this union (*maithuna*) is known as *nāda*.

*Nādabrahma* : *Nāda* conceived as *Brahman* in the form of primordial sound expressed in *parā*, *paśyanti*, *madhyamā* and *vaikhari*.

*Nāḍī* : Nerves of the human body. Pulse.

*Nīlakaṇṭha* : Blue throat (Śiva).

*Nirañjana* : Speckless.

*Nirguṇa* : Attributeless.

*Nirmāṇa-kāya* : Noumenal body.

*Nirvāṇa* : Non-duality; Salvation.

*Nivṛtti* : Return current.

*Nyāsa* : Identifying deities in different parts of the body of the devotee.

*Pada* : Word.

| | | |
|---|---|---|
| *Pāṇigrahaṇa* | : | Marriage. |
| *Panth* | : | Way; cult. |
| *Parā* | : | Higher knowledge. |
| *Parabrahman* | : | Supreme being; the absolute; the ultimate reality in the form of pure consciousness. |
| *Parakīyā* | : | Female partner of the aspirant who is not his own wife; unconventional. |
| *Parama haṃsa* | : | The one who has attained success in *haṃsa mantra.* |
| *Paramānanda* | : | Supreme bliss. |
| *Paramasukha* | : | Non-duality. |
| *Parameśvara* | : | Supreme Lord. |
| *Parameśvarī* | : | Goddess conceived as supreme being. |
| *Parā-śabda* | : | Motionless causal sound. |
| *Parā-śakti* | : | *Parā-śakti* is the energy of Śiva which is regarded as the instrumental cause of creation. The term is also used to denote the power of independence of the supreme being. In the *Śaiva* and *Śākta* outlook, *parā-śakti* is the *vimarśa*, that is, vibrating or kinetic energy of the supreme being. It is equated with *kuṇḍalinī* and its functioning. |
| *Parā vāk* | : | It is the first stage of sound expressing itself only at *mūlādhāra.* It is without any vibration. It is like a flame of light, unmanifested yet indestructible. |
| *Pāśa* | : | Fetters. |
| *Paśu* | : | Fettered individual. |
| *Paśu bhāva* | : | Ordinary human state. |
| *Paśyanti* | : | One of the constituents of sound, it is |

regarded as the second stage of its development. This form of sound belongs to the naval region. It has little vibration and is connected with *nādatattva*.

*Piṅgalā* : One of the major nerves. Together with its sister nerve *iḍā* it rises from *mūlādhāra* and ends in the right nostril. It is also known as *Sūrya-nāḍī*—having the masculine characteristics of the sun.

*Prajñā* : Insight; knowledge; wisdom.

*Prakāśa* : The state of the ultimate reality.

*Prakṛti* : Female Principle of creation, variously conceived of as primordial matter or energy. Often identified with Śakti, the supreme being of the *Śāktas*; mature.

*Pralaya* : Dissolution (*saṁhāra*).

*Prāṇa/Apāna* : Vital wind.

*Prāṇamaya-kośa* : Sheath of life.

*Prasāda* : Divine grace.

*Pravṛtti* : Moving onward.

*Pṛthvī* : Earth.

*Pūjā* : Worship.

*Puṇya* : Merit.

*Puruṣa-Prakṛti* : Male and Female Principles of creation, later equated with the principles of sound and matter.

*Puruṣārtha* : *Dharma* (religion), *artha* (money); *kāma* (desire), *mokṣa* (liberation) are the four *puruṣārthas*.

*Pūrva* : Earlier.

| | | |
|---|---|---|
| *Rāga* | : | Attachment; emotion. |
| *Rasa* | : | Taste, sap, elixir, sentiment. *Rasa* is also conceived in terms of intense emotional attachment between the Male and Female Principles, symbolising two aspects of Śakti and impersonated by the aspirant and his partner. |
| *Recaka* | : | A form of breath-control. |
| *Ṛṇas* | : | Debts. |
| *Rūpa* | : | Form. |
| *Śabda* | : | Sound; word. |
| *Śabda-brahma* | : | *Brahman* or *Śakti* conceived as the substratum of sound. **See** under *Parā*, *Paśyanti*, *Madhyamā* and *Vaikhari*. |
| *Sādhaka* | : | Spiritual aspirant; seeker. |
| *Sādhanā* | : | Term for spiritual exercise. |
| *Sādhya* | : | To be sought. |
| *Saguṇa* | : | With attributes. |
| *Sahaja* | : | (a) The way (*mārga*) of spiritual exercise which is the earliest and most natural. It is also the term for ultimate reality among the *Sahajīyas*, i.e., those who believe in this *mārga*.<br>(b) Non-duality. |
| *Sahajānand* | : | Non-duality. |
| *Sahasrāra* | : | The highest cerebral region above; all the *cakras* or nerve-plexuses where *kuṇḍalinī* meets its source. For its description ***see*** *Ṣaṭcakranirūpaṇa*, XLI-XLIII. |
| *Śakti* | : | Energy; female partner of the aspirant; it |

is the power of the supreme being conceived as the Female Principle through which the manifestation of the universe is effected. The important aspects of this power are *cit* (will), *jñāna* (knowledge) and *kriyā* (action).

*Sālokya* : This is one of the four stages of beatitude.

*Samādhi* : State of perfect bliss in which the world of senses disappears from the mind of the aspirant. It is the aim of all yogic exercises — non-duality.

*Sāmantabhadra* : Entirely auspicious.

*Samarasa* : The state of unity of emotion.

*Sāmarasya* : Equilibrium of Śiva and Śakti, Male and Female Principles. In Buddhism it is that of *upāya* and *prajñā*. Very often this equilibrium is conceived of in sexual terms. Its spirit is felt by the aspirant within his own self. Complete understanding of this equilibrium leads to the experience of non-duality.

*Sambhoga-kāya* : Body of Bliss.

*Sāmīpya* : This is one of the four stages of beatitude; proximity (in space and time).

*Saṁsāra* : World.

*Saṁskāra* : Impression.

*Sanjñā* : Perception.

*Saṅkleśa* : Adherence.

*Sārūpya* : Conformity with the deity; one of the grades of *mukti* or beatitude.

*Sat* : Existence.

| | | |
|---|---|---|
| *Ṣaṭcakra* | : | The six nerve-plexuses, i.e., *mūlādhāra, svādhiṣṭhāna, maṇipūra, anāhata, viśuddha* and *ājñā*. |
| *Śava* | : | Corpse. |
| *Siddha-siddhi* | : | *Siddhi* is spiritual attainment. The term is also used to denote the attainment of miraculous power. He or she who has attained *siddhi* is known as *siddha*. |
| *Śiṣya* | : | Disciple. |
| *Skandha* | : | Elements. |
| *Spanda* | : | Motion. |
| *Sparśa* | : | Touch. |
| *Śrīyantra* | : | The most important Tāntric diagram connected with the cult of Śrīvidyā. It is also known as *śrīcakra* and *tripura-cakra*. This diagram symbolises the body of the goddess. It consists of nine triangles or *yoni*, five in the name of Śakti and four in that of Śiva. The Śakti-triangles are pointed upwards and the Śiva-triangles downwards. |
| *Sṛṣṭi* | : | Creation. |
| *Sthāna* | : | Place. |
| *Sthiti* | : | Substance. |
| *Sthūla* | : | Gross. |
| *Sthūla-deha (śarīra)* | : | Gross body. |
| *Sukha* | : | Bliss. |
| *Sūkṣma-deha (śarīra)* | : | Subtle body. |
| *Śūnya* | : | Reality. |

*Śūnyatā* : Perfect knowledge; void; the Buddhist idea of vacuity conceived of in terms of the female principle. It is also known as *prajñā* and symbolised in the form of different goddesses. The male principle is thought of as *karuṇā* or *upāya*.

*Sūrya* : Sun.

*Suṣumnā* : The most important nerve, also known as *brahmanāḍī*. It is said that universe itself is contained in this nerve. It extends from the *mūlādhāra* to *brahmarandhra*. It is the route by which *kuṇḍalinī* marches upwards.

*Suṣupti* : Sleep.

*Svādhiṣṭhāna* : The nerve-plexus situated above the *mūlādhāra*.

*Svakīyā* : Conjugal; female partner who is the valid wife of the aspirant.

*Svapna* : Illusion; dream.

*Svecchayā* ; Own free will.

*Tattva* : Essential principles.

*Tirobhāva* or *Tirodhāna* : Concealment.

*Trikoṇa* : Triangle, also known as *yoni*; female generative organ.

*Trinetra* : With three eyes (Śiva).

*Turīya* : A very high state. The *sahasrāra cakra* is supposed to contain a field of knowledge which is also known as *turīya*.

*Upāsanā* : Worship.

*Upāya* : Method or means.

| | | |
|---|---|---|
| *Uttara* | : | Later. |
| *Vācaka/Vācya* | : | Śakti or power of *mantra*; the former is the denoting or signifying aspect, while the later is the basic one. *Vācya* is contained in the *vācaka* and formally there is no distinction between them. |
| *Vaikhari* | : | One of the four ingredients of sound, the others being *parā*, *paśyahti* and *madhyamā*. It is that sound which is carried by the wind inside the body and becomes articulated in the throat. It is the gross sound. |
| *Vajra* | : | Thunderbolt. |
| *Vajrayāna* | : | A form of Tāntric Buddhism. |
| *Vāk* | : | Speech. |
| *Vāmā* | : | Woman. |
| *Varṇātmaka* | : | |
| *Vāyu* | : | Wind. |
| *Vedanā* | : | Feeling. |
| *Vidyā* | : | Denotes knowledge. |
| *Vijñāna* | : | Ego-consciousness/consciousness. |
| *Vijñānamaya-kośa* | : | Sheath of higher mind. |
| *Vimarśakhya* | : | Differentiating aspect. |
| *Vindu* | : | A term used in a variety of senses. As a dot denotes Śiva and as a double dot (*visarga*), Śakti, both being alphabetical signs. The former stands for solar power, the later for lunar. In *Śaiva* conception, *vindu* is an evolute of *nāda* which is produced owing to the *kriyā-śakti* of Śiva. It also stands for the male organ |

| | | |
|---|---|---|
| | | while *visarga* denotes the female organ. |
| *Vīra* | : | Tāntric aspirant of the second grade whose mental faculties are of advanced nature. |
| *Visarga* | : | Alphabetical sign of double-dot which is symbolically regarded as the complementary Śakti of *vindu*. It signifies both the *parā* and *aparā* aspects of Śakti. It is the female principle (*saḥ*) as complementary to the male principle (*haṃ*). |
| *Viśuddha* | : | The nerve-plexus above the *anāhat* in the neck. |
| *Viśvādhik* | : | More than the universe. |
| *Viśvamāyā* | : | Immanent. |
| *Viśvarūpa* | : | The form of the universe. |
| *Viśvottīrṇa* | : | Transcendent. |
| *Vyakta* | : | Manifest or form. |
| *Vyavadhāna* | : | Distinction. |
| *Yāmala* | : | Non-duality. |
| *Yāna* | : | Way (Paths). |
| *Yantra* | : | Symbol of deity. It is generally the form of diagram or geometrical pattern serving as a chart for revealing the characteristics of the deity. |
| *Yoga* | : | Disciplining of the body for various purposes — physical, mental and spiritual and meditation. |
| *Yoganidrā* | : | (a) Sleep personified as a goddess and said to be the form of Durgā.<br>(b) The great sleep of Brahmā during the |

period between the annihilation and reproduction of the universe.

*Yoni* : Female generative organ.

*Yugal* : Non-duality.

*Yuganaddha* : Male principle in union with the female principle. It is the non-dual state of unity of *śūnyatā* and *karuṇā*.

# Index

*abheda*, 76
*ācāra*, 57
*ācārya*, 6
*adhisavana*, 60
Ādi Buddha, 83, 112
Ādinātha, 93, 96
*ādiśūnya*, 95
*advaita*, 29, 30, 55
*advaita-vedānta*, 30, 33, 55
*advaya*, 59, 83
*ādyā śakti*, 29
*āgama*, 36, 41, 43
*aghora*, 13, 66
*aghori*, 84
*aghoritāntrika*, 40
Agni, 23, 28
Aihole, 105
*aikya*, 33
Ajantā, 103, 105
*ājñā*, 70, 95
*ājñācakra*, 50, 68, 69
*ākāśa*, 71
*akṣobhya*, 82
*alakha-nirañjana*, 84
*alasa kanyā*, 16
*amar*, 35
*Amarakośa*, 35
Ambernāth, 109
Ambikā, 17
Amitābha, 82
*amoghasiddhi*, 82
*amṛta*, 94, 95, 96
*anādi*, 93
*anāhata*, 50, 68, 70, 95
*anāhata cakra*, 69, 87
*ānanda*, 25, 31, 32, 55, 59, 60, 65, 66
*ānandamayakośa*, 50, 73
*ānandaśakti*, 31
*aṅga*, 33
*annamaya-kośa*, 50
*aṅśa*, 33
*antaḥ śūnya*, 95
*antarātmā*, 69
*anugraha*, 34
*anuttara*, 30
*anuttara yoga tantra*, 82, 83
*apāna*, 45, 88, 93, 95
*apāna-vāyu*, 46
*aparā*, 28
*ardhanārīśvara*, 46, 69
*artha*, 41, 71, 72, 108

*asṛja*, 76
*aṣṭakoṇa*, 76
*asthi*, 76
*Atharvaveda*, 13, 17, 23, 24, 60, 96
*ātmā*, 53, 58
*ātmadarśana*, 44
*ātman*, 30, 33
*ātmaśakti*, 44
*ātmatattva*, 74
*avadhūti*, 86, 88, 92
*avidyā*, 28, 33, 66
*avyakta*, 44, 71
*avyaktarūpa*, 13
*Āyurveda*, 51

Bādāmī, 105
*bahiścarman*, 60
Bāṇa, 104, 107
Bāṇabhatta, 35
*baṅk-nāla*, 95
Bhadra Kālī, 17
Bhagavatī, 85
Bhairava, 14, 15, 40, 67
*bhakti*, 25, 27, 34, 57, 97, 99
*bhāṇḍa*, 93
*bharaṇa*, 15
Bhārhut, 103
Bhāsa, 105
*bhāṣya*, 20
*bhāva*, 50, 71, 77
Bhavabhūti, 107
Bhavānī, 17
*bhīmā*, 28
*bhīṣana*, 15
*bhoga*, 90, 91, 111
Bhuddhahood, 81, 85, 96, 99
*bhūta*, 24, 64
Bhuvanīśvara, 105, 109, 110
Bhuvanīśvari, 75
*bīja*, 18, 19, 55 69, 72, 96
*bīja-mantra*, 41, 70
*bindu*, 19, 43, 44, 50, 53, 55, 69, 72, 76, 77
*bindu-dhāraṇa*, 94
*bindu-siddhi*, 84
*bodhicitta*, 59, 85, 87, 88, 90, 96
*bodhisattva*, 82, 84, 99, 112
Brahmā, 14, 17, 26, 57, 107
*Brahman*, 24, 26, 29, 32, 33, 36, 39, 54, 57, 58, 65, 73, 77, 98
Brāhmaṇa, 40, 60, 64, 97, 103
*brahmāṇḍa*, 93
*brahmāṇḍaraśana*, 20
Brāhmaṇical, 5, 6, 27
Brāhmaṇical-Hinduism, 18, 19
Brāhmaṇism, 38
*brahmāṅśaṅsparśa*, 20
*brahmānubhava*, 20
*brahmarandhra*, 69
*Brahma Sūtra*, 20
*Bṛhadāraṇyaka Upaniṣad*, 51, 60
*Bṛhat-saṁhitā*, 35
Buddha, 16, 26, 39, 51, 80, 81, 83, 84, 86, 90, 92, 99, 100, 112
*buddhi*, 50
Buddhism, 5, 6, 18, 26, 27, 29, 38, 80, 81, 83, 86, 87, 96, 100, 103, 110, 112

Buddhist, 18, 79 80, 81, 99, 100, 102, 103, 105, 106, 107, 110
Buddhist-Brahmā, 112
Buddhistic, 86
Buddhist-*sahajīyā*, 84
Buddhist-*tantra*, 13, 39, 75, 81, 83, 84, 85, 86, 92, 93, 96
Buddhist-tāntrism, 96, 110

*caitanya*, 30, 35
*cakra*, 6, 15, 19, 46, 68, 70, 72, 75, 76, 77, 85, 87, 92, 96
*cakra-pūjā*, 84, 109
*cakra-puruṣa*, 15
Cāmuṇḍā, 28
*candāli*, 86, 88
Caṇḍī, 28
Caṇḍikā, 28
*candra*, 94
*candra-maṇḍala*, 69
Cārvāka, 26
*caryā*, 18
*caryā-tantra*, 82
*catuṣpada*, 75
*Chāndogya Upaniṣad*, 60, 61
Chinnamastā, 11
*cit*, 31, 32, 34, 55, 65, 66
*cit-śakti*, 31, 56, 92
*citta-bhūmi*, 89
*citta nirodha*, 94

Ellorā, 105

*gāṇapatya*, 56
Gaṇeśa, 15
Gaṅgā, 88
Gautam Buddha, 26
*goṣṭhī*, 104
*grāhaka*, 71, 90
*grāhya*, 71, 90
Guhya, 81
Guhyasamāja, 81
Gujarata, 106, 107
*guṇa*, 34, 71
Gupta, 100
*guru*, 37, 57, 89, 91, 94
*gurutattva*, 57

Hairuka, 15
Halebid, 109
*haṁsa*, 69, 95
Hanu-Bhairava, 15
Hara-Gaurī, 95
*Harivaṁśa*, 35
*haṭhayoga*, 45, 92, 96, 110
*haṭha yogic*, 110
*Hevajra tantra*, 90
*hiṁkāra*, 60
*Hīnayāna*, 80, 81
Hindu, 5, 18, 19, 20, 66, 79, 84, 86, 98, 100, 102, 103, 105, 106, 107, 110, 112
Hinduism, 6, 18, 80, 87, 110
Hindu-tantra, 87, 92, 96
Hiraṇyagarbha, 11

*icchā*, 66, 73, 76
*icchā-śakti*, 31, 66
*iḍā*, 48, 92, 93

*iśāna*, 13, 23, 66

Jaiminīya Brāhmaṇa, 60, 73
Jain, 18, 93, 99, 102, 103, 106, 107, 110
Jainism, 5, 6, 18, 26, 27, 38, 110
*jīva*, 33, 53, 54, 56, 76, 77
*jīvan-mukta*, 59
*jīvan-mukti*, 74
*jñāna*, 18, 25, 28, 55, 57, 58, 66, 76
*jñāna-śākti*, 31, 66, 76

Kadwana, 109
Kailāsanāth, 105
*kaivalya*, 25
*kalā*, 34, 66, 69
*kāla*, 15
*kālacakra*, 83
*kālacakratantra*, 83
*kālacakrayāna*, 83
*kālāgni*, 94
*kālāmukha*, 106, 110
Kālī, 28, 75
Kālidāsa, 107
Kālikā, 12, 13
Kalyāṇa Sunder, 14
*kāma*, 11, 12, 60, 61, 108
*kāma-bīja*, 68
*kāma-kalā*, 19
*kāma kalā nāda*, 72
*kamala*, 59
*Kāmasūtra*, 104
*kāma-vāyu*, 68
Kāmeśvara, 76
Kameśvarī, 75
*kanaphaṭayogī*, 93
Ḱānherī, 103
*kāpālika*, 84
Kapgallu, 101
Karāli, 28
*kāraṇa śarīra*, 50
Kārli, 103
*karma*, 26, 27, 28, 33, 94, 97
*karuṇā*, 53, 83, 85, 87
Kāśmir, 106
Kāśmir-Śaivism, 30
Kāśyapa, 81
*Kaṭha Upaniṣad*, 20, 34
*kaula*, 39, 57, 59, 68, 83, 84
*kaulācāra*, 39, 67
*kaula mārga*, 92
*kaulastrī*, 67
Kauśalyā, 15
*Kauśitaki Brāhmaṇa*, 60, 73
*kavaca*, 79
*kāyā*, 19
*kāya-sādhanā*, 93, 94, 95
*Kena Upaniṣad*, 20
Khajurāho, 100, 107, 109, 110
*khila*, 102
*klīṁ*, 68
Koṇārka, 100
*kriyā*, 18, 66, 73, 76
*kriyā-śakti*, 31, 66, 72
*kriyā-tantra*, 82
Kṛṣṇa, 11
*kṣobhya*, 55
*kula*, 39

*kula-kuṇḍalinī*, 50
*kulapatha*, 68
*Kulārṇava Tantra*, 38, 52, 58, 67
*kuṇḍala*, 93
*kuṇḍalinī*, 5, 11, 19, 56, 58, 68, 71, 72, 84, 92
*kuṇḍalinī-rūpa*, 72
*kuṇḍalinī-śakti*, 68, 72, 73, 86
*kuṇḍalini-yoga*, 73
Kuṣāṇa, 104

Lakṣmī, 36
*lalanā*, 85, 92
Lalitā, 75, 76, 77
*līlā*, 49
*liṅga*, 13, 33, 70, 109
*liṅgam*, 109
*liṅgāṅga sāmarasya*, 33
*liṅga-yoni*, 16
Lomāni, 60

*madhyama*, 54
*madhyamā*, 41, 71, 73
*madhyamā viśeṣa spanda*, 71
*Mādhyamika*, 82, 95
*madhyaśūnya*, 95
*madirā*, 38, 61
*mahā-bhūta*, 64
*mahā-rāga*, 86
Mahādevī, 12
Mahākāla, 15
Mahākūṭeśvara, 105
Mahālakṣmī, 29
*mahāmāyā*, 66
*mahānirvāṇatantra*, 36
*mahāpuruṣalakṣanas*, 99
*mahārasa*, 94
*mahāsāṅghika*, 99
*mahāsukha*, 38, 59, 83, 85, 86, 88, 89, 93
*Mahāsukhasthāna*, 92, 93
*mahāvidyā*, 66
Mahāvīra, 26, 39
*Mahāyāna*, 80, 81, 112
Mahāyānic *karuṇā*, 95
Mahāyānist, 99
Maheśvara, 29, 76, 94
Maheśvarī, 17
*maithuna*, 38, 39, 58, 59, 60, 61, 73, 100, 102, 103, 104, 105, 106, 108, 111
*majjā*, 76
*makāra*, 38, 64, 67, 84, 111
*māṁsa*, 38, 61, 76
*manas*, 69
*mānasatīrtha*, 16
*maṇḍala*, 15, 18, 68, 79, 84, 111
*maṇḍapa*, 105
Māṇḍūkyopaniṣad, 14
*maṇipūra cakra*, 50, 68, 70
*maṇipūrak cakra*, 87, 95
Mañjuśrī, 15
Mañjuśrīmūlakalpa, 18
*manomaya-kośa*, 50
*mantra*, 5, 28, 35, 38, 54, 58, 71, 72, 79, 83, 84
*mantrayāna*, 83
*Manu-smṛti*, 73
Maruta, 23

Mathurā, 104
*mātṛkā*, 71, 72
*matsya*, 38, 61
*māyā*, 12, 29, 33, 36, 66, 73, 74, 76
*māyin*, 29
*medā*, 76
*Mithuna*, 43, 106, 111
*moharātri*, 29
*mokṣa*, 32, 43, 84, 99, 108, 111
Mṛtyuñjaya, 11
*mudrā*, 18, 38, 61, 73, 80, 84
*mukha-liṅga*, 13
*mukhaliṅgam*, 105
*mukti*, 25
*mūla*, 69
*mūlādhāra*, 46, 68, 70, 72, 93
*mūlādhāra-cakra*, 6, 19, 50, 67, 68, 71, 95
*mūla-prakṛti*, 33
*Muṇḍaka Upaniṣad*, 34, 73
*muṇḍamālā*, 12
*muskāna*, 60
Mysore, 101, 106

*nāda*, 19, 41, 43, 44, 50, 53, 55, 72
*nāḍī*, 51, 73, 76, 92
Nālandā, 110
Nāsik, 103
*Nātha*, 91, 93, 94, 96
*nātha-panthī*, 84, 109
*Nātha siddha*, 94, 96
Nāthism, 83, 94, 95
Nāthist, 39, 40
*nāyaka*, 40
*nidhāna*, 61
*nigama*, 43
*nirañjana*, 93
*nirguṇa*, 34, 55
*nirmāṇa*, 86
*nirmāṇa-cakra*, 86, 87, 88
*nirmāṇa-kāya*, 87, 100
*nirvāṇa*, 21, 25, 51, 59, 85, 94
*nirvāṇa-kalā*, 69
*nirvāṇa-śakti*, 69
*niśka*, 23
*Niṣpannayogāvalī*, 18
*nivṛtti*, 46, 54, 87, 90
*nyāsas*, 18

*Oṁ*, 14, 61
Orissa, 107

*pada*, 71
*padma*, 70, 76
Pahārpura, 110
*pañca-makāra*, 64, 67
*pañcamukhaliṅga*, 13
*pañcarātra*, 18
*pañcatattva*, 54
*pañcopāsanā*, 56
*pāṇigrahaṇa*, 14
*panth*, 91
*parā*, 28, 41, 71, 72, 73
*parā-bindu*, 69
*parabrahman*, 65
*parakīyā*, 89
*parama*, 68
*paramānanda*, 13

*parama Śiva*, 69
*paramasukha*, 59
*parameśvara*, 30, 33
*pāramitās*, 99
*parāmṛta śakti*, 77
*parā-nāda*, 72
*parā-śabda*, 71
*parā-śakti*, 32, 33, 58, 72
*parā saṁvit*, 30
*parā Śiva*, 58
Paraśurāmeśvara, 105
*parā-vāc*, 72
Pārśvanāth, 107
Pārthian, 104
Pārvatī, 14, 36
*paśu*, 54, 111
*paśubhāva*, 57
*paśupata*, 101, 106, 109, 110
*Paśupati*, 101
*paśyanti*, 41, 71, 73
Patañjali, 107
*pati-pāśa-paśu*, 30
Paṭṭadakala, 105
*pavananiścāñcalya*, 94
*pavitratā*, 75
*piṅgalā*, 46, 48, 92, 93
*prajñā*, 29, 53, 59, 81, 83, 85, 86, 87, 88, 89, 95, 109
*prajñāpāramitā*, 14, 18
*prajñopāya*, 88
*prakāśa*, 74
*prakāśaka*, 71
*prakāśya*, 71
*prakṛti*, 14, 28, 34, 36, 40, 44, 50, 53, 55, 64, 67, 74
*pralaya*, 31, 33, 34, 55
*prāṇa*, 45, 76, 88, 93, 95
*prāṇamayakośa*, 50
*prasāda*, 27
*prastāva*, 61
*pratihāra*, 61
*pratyabhijñā*, 30
*pravṛtti*, 46, 87
primal, 14
*pṛthivī*, 49
*pṛthivītattva*, 68
*pūjā*, 98
*puṇya*, 106
*Purāṇa*, 36, 106
Purāṇic, 17
Purāṇic Hinduism, 105
*puruṣa*, 14, 28, 44, 53, 60, 64, 67, 103
*puruṣa-prakṛti*, 17
*puruṣārtha*, 108
*pūrva*, 39

Rādhā, 36
*rāga*, 86
Rāghavabhaṭṭ, 72
*raja*, 34
*rajoguṇa*, 12
Rāma, 15
*rasa*, 70
*rasanā*, 85, 92
*rati*, 11, 12, 13
Ratnāgiri, 107
*rātra*, 36
*ṛddhi*, 91

*Ṛgveda*, 13, 23, 24, 59, 60, 61, 73, 96, 102
Ṛgvedic, 17, 23, 24
*ṛṇa*, 24
*ṛṣi*, 20
Rudra, 23, 33
*rudrākṣa*, 93
Rudra-Śiva, 23, 33
*rūpa*, 70, 82, 86

*śabda*, 41, 68, 70, 71, 72
*śabda-brahman*, 55
*saccidānanda*, 54
Sadāśiva, 69, 76
*Saddharmapuṇḍarīka*, 18
*sādhaka*, 6, 11, 12, 19, 44, 46, 50, 54, 56, 59, 77, 83, 89, 91, 92, 96, 98, 100
*sādhanā*, 5, 44, 45, 46, 53, 54, 55, 56, 59, 79, 86, 88, 91, 92, 108, 110, 111
*Sādhanamālā*, 18
*sādhya*, 44
*sadyojāta*, 13, 66
*saguṇa*, 55
*saguṇa Brahman*, 30
*sahaja*, 59, 68, 83, 86, 87, 89, 90, 92, 93, 109, 111
*sahaja-kāya*, 86
*sahaja-mahā-sūkha*, 89
Sahajānanda, 59
*Sahajayāna*, 83
*sahajīya*, 84
*Sahajīya* Buddhism, 86, 87
*Sahajīya* Buddhist, 87
*sahasrāra*, 6, 46, 50, 58, 67, 68, 69, 70, 72, 86, 93, 94, 95
*sahasrāra cakra*, 96
*Śaiva*, 28, 29, 36, 39, 56, 57, 93, 107
*Śaiva-āgama*, 18, 40
*Śaiva-siddhāntin*, 10
Śaivism, 24, 26, 27, 29, 30, 34
Śaivites, 5
*śaka*, 104
*Śākta*, 5, 18, 26, 28, 39, 56, 63, 64, 65, 86, 93, 107
*Śākta Tantra*, 40, 86
*Śakti*, 11, 18, 19, 28, 29, 30, 31, 32, 33, 35, 36, 38, 39, 40, 43, 44, 46, 49, 53, 54, 55, 56, 57, 58, 59, 63, 65, 66, 67, 68, 69, 71, 72, 74, 75, 76, 77, 81, 87, 93, 95, 96, 100, 109, 112
*śaktinipāta*, 32
Śāktism, 29, 36, 63, 64, 65, 66, 84
*sālokya*, 32
*samādhi*, 59, 81, 89
*sāmanta*, 105
*sāmantabhadra*, 88
*sāmānya-spanda*, 71
*samarasa*, 59, 85, 86, 89
*sāmarasya*, 68
*Sāmaveda*, 24
*sāmayin*, 39
*saṁbhoga*, 86
*saṁbhoga cakra*, 86, 87
*saṁbhoga-kāya*, 87, 100
Saṁbhu, 30
*saṁhāra*, 34

*Saṁhitā*, 36
*sāmīpya*, 32
*Sāṁkhya*, 17, 26, 27, 28, 35, 40 44, 53, 54, 67, 74
*saṁsāra*, 32, 33
*saṁskāra*, 82
*saṅgīti*, 81
*sanjñā*, 82
Śaṅkara, 20
Saṅkhinī, 95
*saṅkleśa*, 90
*sapand*, 30
*Sāradā Tilak*, 72, 78
*sārūpya*, 32
Sarasvatī, 28
*sarya*, 16, 75
*śāstra*, 55
*sat*, 32, 34, 65
*śatadala kamal*, 16
*Śatapatha Brāhmaṇa*, 60, 73
*ṣaṭcakrabheda*, 67
*sattva*, 34
*saumya*, 14
*śava*, 19, 67
*siddha*, 25, 71, 91, 92
*siddhācārya*, 91
*siddhānta*, 57
*siddhāntācāra*, 67
*siddhi*, 55, 91, 111
*Śilpa*, 102
Śiva, 11, 12, 14, 15, 19, 23, 26, 28, 29, 30, 31, 32, 33, 34, 36, 46, 49, 53, 54, 55, 57, 58, 59, 66, 67, 68, 74, 75, 76, 84, 87, 93, 95, 96, 101, 109
Śiva-*kāma*, 75
*Śivaliṅga*, 13, 101
Śivarātri, 93
Śiva-Śakti, 29, 72
Śiva-*tattva*, 31, 74
*skandha*, 82
*smṛti*, 36
*soma*, 60, 94, 95
Somanāthpura, 109
Someśvara, 105
*sparśa*, 70
*Śrī*, 102
*Śrīcakra*, 39
Śrī-Lakṣmī, 75
Śrī Lalitā, 77
*Śrī-sūkta*, 102
*sṛṣṭi*, 19, 31, 33, 34
*sthiti*, 34
*sthūla*, 56
*strāṇa*, 35
*suddha vidyā*, 76
Śūdraka, 104
*sukha*, 89
Sukhāvati, 85, 90
*śukra*, 76
*śukram*, 90
*summum-bonum*, 85
*śūnya*, 80, 82, 83, 85, 93, 95
*śūnyatā*, 53, 83, 87, 95
*śūnya-vāda*, 95
*Sūrya*, 23, 56, 69, 88, 94
Suśruta, 3
*suṣumnā*, 48, 68
*suṣumnā-nāḍī*, 69

*svādhiṣṭhāna*, 50, 68, 70, 92
*svādhiṣṭhāna-cakra*, 68
*svakīyā*, 89
*svastika*, 69
*svātantrya*, 31
*svayaṁbhu liṅga*, 68
*svecchayā*, 31
*Śvetāsvatara Upaniṣad*, 24, 73

*Taittirīya Āraṇyaka*, 61
*Taittirīya Upaniṣad*, 51
*tam*, 34
*tan*, 35
*tantra*, 5, 6, 17, 18, 29, 35, 36, 38, 39, 40, 41, 43, 44, 45, 46, 53, 54, 55, 56, 57, 59, 64, 71, 74, 79, 80, 81, 87, 89, 99
*tantrī*, 35
tāntric, 5, 6, 18, 19, 29, 36, 40, 43, 45, 46, 49, 50, 53, 61, 63, 64, 65, 66, 70, 75, 77, 80, 82, 84, 85, 93, 100, 110
tāntric Buddhism, 84
tāntric Buddhist, 79
tāntric Jain, 107
tāntric *maithuna*, 60
tāntric *sādhaka*, 57
tāntric *sādhanā*, 45, 59, 71, 84, 112
tāntric Śaivism, 112
tāntric *yoga*, 91
*tāntrika*, 54, 57, 109, 110, 111, 112
Tāntrism, 5, 59, 64, 79, 80, 86, 101, 106, 109, 110, 112
*tatpuruṣa*, 13, 66
*tatrī*, 35
*tattva*, 31, 39, 46, 55, 58, 61, 70, 76
Ter, 101
*tirobhāva*, 34
*tirodhāna*, 34
*tīrtha*, 16
*tīrthaṅkara*, 99
*trika*, 30
*trikoṇa*, 15, 70
*tripuṇḍra*, 93
Tripurasundarī, 75
*tvak*, 76

*udgītha*, 61
Umā, 17, 33
*Upaniṣad*, 15, 24, 25, 26, 27, 28, 39, 60, 61, 64, 68, 73, 107
Upaniṣadic, 29, 107
*upāsanā*, 77, 111
*upastha*, 60
*upāya*, 53, 59, 85, 86, 87,88
*Ūrdhva-liṅga*, 13
*uṣṇīśa kamala*, 86, 87, 88, 96
*uttar*, 39

*vāc*, 17, 22
*vācaka*, 19, 71
*vācya*, 19, 71
*vaikhānasa*, 18
*vaikharī*, 41, 71, 73
Vaiṣṇava, 28, 36, 39, 56, 57, 93, 107
*Vaiṣṇava-āgama*, 18
*Vaiṣṇava Saṁhitā*, 40

Vaiṣṇavism, 26, 27, 29, 99, 112
Vaiṣṇavites, 5
*vajra*, 59, 82, 85
*vajra kanyā*, 85, 86
*vajra-path*, 82
*vajra-sattva*, 96
*Vajrayāna*, 83, 112
Vajrayāna Buddhism, 80
Vajrayāna Buddhist, 89
Vajrayānic *upāya*, 95
*vāk*, 28, 40
*vākya*, 71
*vāma*, 57
*vāmā*, 54, 57
*vāmācāra*, 40, 54, 55, 67, 84, 101
Vāmadeva, 13, 66
*vāmadiyasāmanas*, 61
*vāma-mārga*, 92
*varṇātmaka-śabda*, 71
Vātsyāyana, 104
*vāyu-maṇḍala*, 69
*Veda*, 26, 27, 36, 57, 97, 98
*vedanā*, 82
*Vedānta*, 28, 53, 54, 73
Vedāntic, 36
*vedī*, 60
Vedic, 20, 25, 27, 28, 40, 53, 54, 60, 61, 63, 64, 70, 97, 98, 101
*vedikā*, 104
*vicikarṣa*, 55
*vidhi*, 110
*vidyā*, 28, 66, 81
*vidyā tattva*, 74
*vijñāna*, 82, 83
*vijñānamaya-kośa*, 50
*vijñānavādins*, 82
*vimarśa*, 74
*vimarśakhya*, 33
*vimarśa prakāśa*, 67
*vīra*, 68, 111
*vīrabhāva*, 57
*virāma-ānanda*, 90
Vīraśaivism, 33
*vīrya*, 84
Viṣṇu, 14, 24, 26, 27, 99
*viśuddha*, 50, 68, 70, 95
*viśuddha cakra*, 69, 87
*viśvādhika*, 34
*viśvamāyā*, 30
*viśvarūpa*, 34
Viśvarūpa Viṣṇu, 15
*viśvotṝṇa*, 30
*vṛtti*, 71, 77
*vyakta*, 13, 44
*vyāpaka-śakti*, 72

*yajña*, 60, 61
*Yajurveda*, 24
*yakṣīs*, 104
*yāmala*, 59
Yamunā, 88
*yāna*, 83
*yantra*, 5, 18, 35, 38, 79, 83
*yoga*, 13, 18, 27, 48, 68, 81, 89, 91, 95, 96
*yoganidrā*, 29
*yoga tantra*, 82, 83
*yogī*, 45, 46, 48, 90, 93, 94, 109

*yogic*, 6, 19, 46, 51, 53, 75, 84, 87, 93, 95
*yogin*, 96
*yoginī*, 40, 110
*yoni*, 64, 68, 70, 109
*yoni-liṅga*, 109
*yoni-paṭṭa*, 13
*yugala*, 59
*yuganaddha*, 13, 59, 84, 85, 86, 90
*yuvatī*, 85